# WHAT TEACHERS NEED TO KNOW ABOUT MEMORY

# WHAT TEACHERS NEED TO KNOW ABOUT MEMORY

JONATHAN FIRTH AND NASIMA RIAZAT

CORWIN

Sage
2455 Teller Road
Thousand Oaks, California 91320
(0800)233-9936
www.corwin.com

Sage
1 Oliver's Yard
55 City Road
London EC1Y 1SP

Sage
Unit No 323-333, Third Floor, F-Block
International Trade Tower Nehru Place
New Delhi 110 019

Sage
3 Church Street
#10-04 Samsung Hub
Singapore 049483

Editor: Amy Thornton
Development editor: Ruth Lilly
Senior project editor: Chris Marke
Cover design: Wendy Scott
Typeset by: C&M Digitals (P) Ltd, Chennai, India
Printed in the UK

**Library of Congress Control Number: 2023937214**

**British Library Cataloguing in Publication Data**

ISBN 978-1-5296-2074-0
ISBN 978-1-5296-2075-7 (pbk)

At Sage we take sustainability seriously. Most of our products are printed in the UK using responsibly sourced papers and boards. When we print overseas we ensure sustainable papers are used as measured by the Paper Chain Project grading system. We undertake an annual audit to monitor our sustainability.

# CONTENTS

# DEDICATION

To my family, for being such great company. You've always supported me and made me laugh, even when I was unwise enough to take on another book project.

*Jonathan*

To my parents Mohammed Riazat (late) and Nasim Akhtar (late) for their unwavering support and belief in the importance of education.

*Nasima*

# ABOUT THE AUTHORS

**Jonathan Firth** is an author, university teacher and researcher. His research interests focus on the psychology of education, specifically memory and teacher professional learning. He has authored several books relating to the psychology of education, as well as school psychology textbooks. He regularly writes articles and blog posts about cognitive science for teachers.

**Nasima Riazat** is a curriculum leader for business studies, vocational learning, careers and PHSE/RSE in a secondary school in the North West. Her PhD is on capacity building and developing leaders. She has written on memory and strategies for teachers and students to use to maximise recall.

# PREFACE

Early in my teaching career, it was unclear to me how to present new material effectively or have a class practise skills in ways that would stick. When students forgot things that they should have known, I didn't know what to do about it. Many readers will have encountered these struggles, too.

It was a lightbulb moment when I realised that my background in cognitive psychology could help tackle these classroom problems. As part of a growing science of learning movement, I gradually came to see that psychology principles could help my practice where more mainstream approaches to CPD had failed. Increasingly, I came to believe that an understanding of memory is relevant to every subject and topic, and to all stages of teaching and learning.

Today, I believe more than ever that this is the case. However, I also recognise that it is hard for many teachers to know how and when to apply memory principles. The aim of this book is to present these concepts in a way that is accurate, accessible and highly practical.

*Jonathan*

With the current trend in education for terminal exam courses requiring students to recall several years' work at the end of the course for their exams, teaching effective strategies about how memory works is one of those things that is becoming increasingly important as part of the teacher's repertoire in supporting students to remember content. Not only the strategies themselves, but a real understanding behind why they work.

As a teacher, I often came across students using ineffective strategies such as highlighting. How to effectively recall course content was something I was increasingly finding myself teaching students about in the classroom alongside the syllabus. This book is designed to support teachers with exploring key ideas around memory and how they can be used to best support your students.

*Nasima*

# 1

# WHAT IS MEMORY?

## INTRODUCTION

Take a moment to consider how you think memory works. How do things that are taught in class enter a student's memory and become part of their knowledge in the future?

Consider the following:

- are learning and memory the same thing?
- how exactly is a new memory taken in, and what happens to it afterwards?
- where does a memory go when it cannot be recalled?
- how is one memory connected to another?
- does it even make sense to talk about 'one' memory, or does each thing we remember depend upon a network of various memories, like a jigsaw puzzle?

What these questions raise is that there are many aspects of memory which can be usefully considered and explored. A commonly made distinction is between long-term memory, for permanent information storage, and working memory, for dealing with information in the here and now for more temporary storage. These forms of memory do different things and work in different ways depending on the task in hand.

This chapter aims to set out key ideas, terms and concepts about memory which will be used throughout the book, and we will explore certain misconceptions which have been found in research about memory. In raising these issues and establishing clear working definitions of regularly used terms in education such as 'memory' and 'learning', the chapter will provide an important bridge between common sense ideas of memory and the more evidence-based approach taken throughout the book.

It is (of course) important to try to explain the nature of memory at the outset of this book. While we all use the word in everyday life, the way scientists define memory may be quite different. As educators, we want to be using the term in ways which are accurate, specific and consistent.

We'll come back to the different types of memory shortly and begin unpick how each of these things work and how they connect together. First, though, let's think about two things that are often treated as synonyms but have important differences, too: memory and learning.

## LEARNING VS MEMORY

Learning is sometimes defined as taking in knowledge and skills in a lasting or permanent way so it can be accessed later, and transferred to new situations (Soderstrom & Bjork, 2015). We think most readers will agree if a learner can't later *access*, *recall* or *use* what they have 'learnt', then they haven't really learnt it at all.

Some educators may view learning as involving something conceptual – a realisation in the moment, perhaps, a breakthrough in understanding. For example, we may say that a student has learnt if they come to understand how the assassination of Archduke Franz Ferdinand of Austria connected to the start of World War I. The teacher may also ask at the end of a lesson, 'what did the pupils learn?', and refer back to broad and conceptual learning intentions.

In contrast, memory is often assumed to be more granular, and more about taking in information. Teachers and students may talk about memorising specific facts, such as names of chemicals in a chemistry lesson, the times tables in primary school, or a process to solve a maths problem, or specific dates in a history lesson.

However, this differs from the psychological definition of long-term memory, which expresses memory as any lasting change in knowledge or skills. It's not confined to simple facts. To take that point a step further, if something has been learnt, for example, a concept, idea, or skill – *there must have been a change in long-term memory that has occurred*. This is just as true for a decision, an analytical thought or a conceptual change of mind as it is for remembering. Coming to understand how key events shaped world history, for example, involves learning, but also memory.

Consider the example in Scenario 1.1 below.

## SCENARIO 1.1

Jade is quite good at most of her subjects, and especially physics and chemistry. On her bus home from school, she has been discussing options for what to do when she finishes school with her friend Pavel. When Pavel points out Jade has always enjoyed discussing politics and social issues, such as world politics, she comes to a realisation. She is good at science, but her true passions lie with the social sciences.

Would we say Jade has learnt anything from this conversation? Arguably, she hasn't taken in any new information. Although it's a simple example, we could say people learn things about themselves from conversations like this. She has reorganised her thoughts and considered something from a new angle. However, such learning also has to be remembered. If Jade didn't retain what she had thought about and remember the decision she had come to, she would be back to square one straight after. She might even end up having the same conversations again and again.

What you begin to see from this discussion are two main things:

1. it's not a simple matter to disconnect learning and memory. These two concepts are closely interlinked;
2. 'common sense' definitions and uses of the term memory are often out of line with science.

To try to unpick the two concepts a little more, it's worth asking a couple more questions:

- could you learn without remembering?
- could you remember without learning?

Hopefully the example in Scenario 1.1 above suggests the answer to the first of these questions is 'no'. If nothing has been retained, then learning *can't* take place – at least, not if we define learning as a relatively lasting process. As well as retaining her decision, Jade's discussion on the bus involved retrieving and linking her thoughts to other details of her school life from her long-term memory and using her working memory to have a conversation.

The answer to the second question could be 'yes'. If we define learning as being about conceptual change and processing things on a deeper level, then an individual could remember something without understanding it – for example, be able to repeat a phrase from a languages lesson but not really understand the meaning behind it.

This is an important point, because some people dismiss memory and the thinking behind what makes memory work because they assume the discussion is all about meaningless memorisation. That's not how we see memory at all. Your memory has the capacity to be used that way, but it's not the best way to use it. As we will see in later chapters, meaningful understanding is important for retaining things well, and for tackling forgetting.

We therefore want to suggest working definitions of these two concepts to cut through these areas of confusion:

- *Memory involves retaining information, skills and knowledge for a period of time.* It is a broader concept than learning.
- *Learning involves lasting conceptual change.* It is underpinned by memory, for any such changes must be retained.

As an analogy, you could consider the difference between dancing and muscles. Dancing is something that we may wish to do. Muscles and other biological systems allow us to do it (and can also be used for other things too). In a similar way, memory is a system which supports learning, and learning can't happen without it.

Learning is the key goal of education, and one that will be a focus throughout. But in order to achieve this goal, teachers like yourself are in the main trying, day by day in lessons, to have an effect on *memory*. Memory can be seen as the key interface that supports conceptual change and breakthroughs in student understanding. This book is about understanding memory and ensuring that we are using it effectively.

## TWO KEY STORES

Two essential terms we have already mentioned are 'working' and 'long-term memory', and it's worth briefly outlining what these are before proceeding further.

## WORKING MEMORY

Working memory is the system which stores and uses of information over a brief period of time. It allows students to retain a small amount of information and/or do something with that information. For example, if a science teacher reads out a list of experimental apparatus to a class and they copy that list into their notebooks, we would say they are using working memory.

As this example illustrates, working memory fades very quickly. Have you ever walked into a room and stopped, wondering why you entered? Or opened a cupboard, only to realise you have forgotten what it was you were intending to look for? In the example of the science lesson, the students will have to copy things into their notebooks a little at a time, demonstrating how brief and limited working memory is.

Working memory can process many types of information and it is not particularly fussy about meaningful understanding at the time of processing, so you could write down a list of five random numbers almost as easily as you could write down a meaningful five-word phrase. In fact, you could probably write down a phrase in a language you don't speak almost as well as one that you do (although you might get the spelling wrong).

That doesn't imply meaning is completely unimportant. In most situations where students use working memory, it is really important they understand what things mean. If a class read and study a passage from *A Christmas Carol* and then select quotes that indicate that Bob Cratchit may be living in poverty, they are using working memory – and also accessing stored knowledge about poverty from long-term memory.

It is worth pointing out at this stage that while memory is sometimes described as a system for retaining *information* (e.g., Gathercole, 1999), for the purposes of this chapter and the book as a whole, the term 'information' should be seen as a neutral and very broad term. Information *might* be relatively meaningless, as some of the examples above show, but more often in learning contexts it will involve meaningful ideas, concepts and skills (for more on this issue, see Chapter 4).

Consider the following examples to better understand what it feels like to use your working memory:

- walking around a large building, counting the windows in each room as you pass them;
- driving a car while having a conversation with the person in the passenger seat.

These examples give us three insights into working memory:

- first, and perhaps most importantly, it is about processing and doing a task in the 'here and now'. It therefore plays a role throughout teaching and learning;

- second, it's clear people can do tasks which are complex, and which include several parts to them, such as visual and verbal information. While working memory is limited in capacity, it has the capacity to cope with two types of information at the same time. For example, a learner may engage with a diagram of photosynthesis in a biology lesson alongside some text to explain the process;
- third, although working memory focuses on the 'now', it involves using stored information too. When we drive, for example, we are using previously learnt knowledge and skills to help understand and respond to 'here and now' experiences.

## LONG-TERM MEMORY

In contrast to working memory, long-term memory (henceforth LTM) is a lasting memory store and can even be permanent. While the everyday tasks we ask our students to do often involve working memory, education is really ultimately about causing lasting changes that affect LTM. We want learners to be able to retain information (to use this term very broadly and neutrally again) over the long term, and to be able to use it in new settings such as for assessments and the world outside school.

It perhaps goes without saying that information is not automatically retained by students. As educators, we need to do things to ensure that new skills and ideas are not forgotten, and that what we teach transfers to new contexts and tasks. The details of how to do this will be a major focus throughout this book; for now, we'll just make a few brief points about the store:

- all learning is underpinned by LTM;
- compared to working memory, LTM is much more dependent on meaningful information;
- LTM is sensitive to context – it's harder to recall information out of context;
- information in LTM is structured into *schemas*, which will be discussed in more detail below;
- LTM is subject to forgetting, but there are things educators can do to significantly reduce forgetting.

Forgetting from LTM has been widely studied for over a century. Indeed, experimental research into this issue dates back to the very first days of experimental psychology. In the late 1800s, researcher Hermann Ebbinghaus discovered that forgetting proceeds rapidly at first and then slows down over time (Ebbinghaus, 1885/1964), as shown in Figure 1.1.

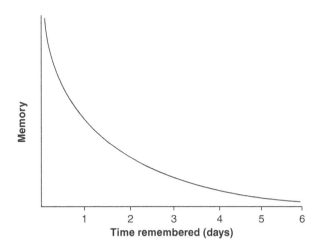

**Figure 1.1**   The forgetting curve

This curve shows a rapid loss of information from memory in the immediate aftermath of learning experiences. We might notice this in a review task at the start of a follow-up lesson, for example. However, it also means that if information can be retained for at least a few weeks, then we can be reasonably confident that it will still be accessible to learners after months or even years. As educators, what happens in those first few days may be crucial to allow this to happen.

It's worth mentioning one other thing at this stage: LTM is not simply a storage vault that information can be randomly thrown into. Instead, new memories are linked to old in structures called *schemas*. A schema is a bundle of knowledge, facts, emotions and actions, and we use these schemas to think about the world. For example, a person's schema for a plane journey may include their knowledge of how a plane works and what it is for, actions such as how to check in or use overhead baggage compartments, as well as emotions such as anxiety.

Schemas have implications which will be discussed throughout this book. For now, it is useful to be aware the more previous background knowledge someone has, the easier it will be to take in and remember new knowledge. An existing schema provides a structure, allowing the learner to make connections and sort the new incoming information. You can consider the existing knowledge as providing pegs to hang new facts upon. In the absence of this prior knowledge, new information will not be understood and mentally categorised, and as a consequence, it will usually be forgotten pretty rapidly.

## REFLECTION POINT

Try to think of a situation where you were told about something, or read about it in a book or online, and struggled to make sense of it due to a lack of background knowledge. For example, perhaps you have read a novel about a war or conflict in another country without knowing much about the social context or the situation prior to the events described.

## PROCESSES OF MEMORY

Now let's think about the process that happens when a learner tries to learn new information. Following the work of psychologists such as Endel Tulving (e.g., Tulving, 1985), taking something into memory is often seen as forming three key processes: encoding, storage and retrieval:

- first, it has to be taken in. This is often called encoding, though you could call it memorisation;
- second, it has to be kept in your memory for a period of time. If a memory is truly forgotten and lost, it can't be of use later. This process is often called storage. As discussed above, storage in working memory is very brief, so in educational contexts, it can be assumed that discussions of storage are usually referring to LTM;
- finally, memories have to be brought back to mind from memory, a process often called retrieval. Again, this is typically discussed in the context of LTM.

We will now consider each of these processes in turn.

## ENCODING

Encoding is where new information enters memory. It can happen as a result of many different tasks or activities such as reading a book, listening to a speaker, or just noticing something for yourself.

We may feel things are going into our memory fairly effortlessly when we hear or see them; however, it worth remembering they are going into working memory, and not necessarily being encoded to the long-term memory.

As educators, it is worth knowing at the planning stage of teaching that encoding to LTM tends to be more effective when students engage in active learning and engage with ideas meaningfully rather than just hearing about them (Wittrock, 1974). We might notice students will often remember a debate or a discussion better than a lecture for this reason. Quizzes can also make learning active, as can activities that prompt learners to compare and categorise material. For example, in citizenship, choosing pieces of information from a text to prioritise into order of importance as to which may influence people to vote is more effective than simply showing a list of possible reasons.

Often, students will try to get things into memory by repetition, or 'rehearsal'. We see this when they reread or copy their notes while studying. Students may focus on a list of definitions or terms, or the lines of a poem, and attempt to repeat these over and over, mentally or out loud. However, repetition is *not* a very effective method of encoding things to memory (see Chapter 3 for more discussion of why this is the case).

## STORAGE

Storage follows on from encoding, and involves retaining things in memory for a period of time. Storage in LTM doesn't require actively thinking about the stored information. In fact, one of the ways you can be sure you are using LTM and not working memory is that you can stop thinking about something for a while, and you don't forget it! Unlike working memory, LTM storage does not depend on holding things in the here and now. As an analogy, you might think of it as your mind's hard drive or filing drawer.

There are important differences between human memory and a hard drive, however. For one thing, memories are quite fragile and they can be changed or distorted by new, incoming information. In addition, storage is not a one-off process. As every teacher knows, it's important to build in opportunities for students to practise, revise and consolidate what has been taken into memory.

## RETRIEVAL

Retrieval is the final stage of the process and involves bringing a memory back to mind from storage. For example, when a student tries to remember how to tackle a trigonometry problem during an exam, they need to retrieve the principles they studied days or months before, perhaps by thinking through the steps they were shown in class.

In an exam, a learner might 'draw a blank', and likewise in everyday life we sometimes forget names, tasks and so on. However, a failure to retrieve memories doesn't always mean that the information has been entirely forgotten. Things can be *in* a person's memory, but that doesn't guarantee that they will be able to recall them when needed.

In experiments, there are three main ways information is retrieved and these have parallels in the classroom:

- *free* recall is when we ask research participants to remember what they can without any help or clues. For example, a participant may be given a blank sheet of paper, and asked to write down all the words they remember seeing on screen during an earlier phase of the experiment, or to try to recreate a text from memory. Due to the absence of support or cues, this is the equivalent of writing an essay in an exam;
- *cued recall* is when we ask research participants to remember things using cues or hints, such as the first letter of a word. This is more like what happens when a teacher asks questions to a class, or prompts learners if they are struggling. It is also similar to gap-fill/close tasks;
- *recognition* is when participants are shown a stimulus, for example a text, word or object, and have to compare it to what they hold in their memory. For example, a researcher might show a word to a participant, and ask, 'Was this word on the list I showed you earlier?' A classroom equivalent would be a multiple-choice task.

## RETRIEVAL PRACTICE

As educators, the three processes explained above are useful when we think about what happens when new information is taken into memory and how it is later retrieved. There is a certain logic to how they link together: something must first be taken into a memory store, then it must be kept in the store and, finally, it must be located and taken out again, similar to the filing cabinet analogy used above.

However, we are still missing important detail on issues like how best to consolidate what has been taken in. We will explore consolidation in a lot of depth in later chapters (see Chapter 3; Chapter 7). For now, it is worth briefly highlighting an important memory strategy that links to all three of the processes above and which can inform the design of almost every type of classroom task: *retrieval practice*.

Retrieval practice involves consolidation of learning through the process of retrieving it from memory in one of the three ways above and, in particular, free recall or cued recall.

At first, it might seem strange to suggest that the process of getting information out of LTM helps with consolidation. Aren't we just taking something out of storage, like getting a file back from a computer hard drive, or a folder from a filing cabinet? However, this illustrates one of the ways that human memory is fundamentally different to a computer. Retrieving a memory *changes that memory*. So, retrieval is not just about getting memories back, but can transform and strengthen the information and/or its connections to other memories. In doing so, engaging in *retrieval* makes the learnt information more resilient and less likely to be forgotten (Agarwal & Bain, 2019; Roediger & Karpicke, 2006).

As a classroom strategy, retrieval practice is strongly associated with the use of short quizzes, direct teacher questioning and revision flashcards. In such situations, learners are forced to actively retrieve what they can. However, there are many other things which could potentially prompt learners to retrieve what they previously learnt, including:

- playing a game where they have to use their past knowledge – for example, practising terminology in a game of hangman;
- writing a 'closed book' essay – for example, in business studies, students might explain strategies such as interest rates used to reduce inflation;
- engaging in a discussion or debate – for example, students may discuss during a PSHE lesson whether the voting age should be changed.

In these and many other situations, learners have to actively retrieve information from LTM. Doing so consolidates that information and makes it easier to remember again in future. They are literally practising the process of recalling it and, as such, these strategies are much more effective than more passive alternatives such as re-reading or hearing a teacher review/summarise a topic.

## MISCONCEPTIONS ABOUT MEMORY

The mid-20th century was the beginning of cognitive psychology as a field. Researchers such as Ulrik Neisser tried to move psychology away from the behaviourist approach and focus more on a person's internal mental processes (e.g., Neisser, 1967). At the same time, early computer scientists were developing systems which stored and manipulated information. These computer programs seemed like the perfect analogy for how the mind works.

However, as the earlier discussion of issues such as storage and retrieval practice suggests, there are certain important features of human memory that don't map particularly well onto computer information processing. Storage in human memory is not a one-off process; without consolidation, information is rapidly lost from LTM in line with Ebbinghaus's forgetting curve. This doesn't apply to computers, which can lose data, but for very different reasons. Computers also don't store information in schemas, linked together with emotions and actions.

These differences bring us onto some popular misconceptions about memory. Even though we all use memory every day, researchers have started to realise people really don't understand their own memories well at all. And these misunderstandings may be leading to flawed approaches to teaching and learning.

## REFLECTION POINT

Consider the following statements – do you agree or disagree?

- Children's minds are like sponges and can take in much more than adults can.
- If a school student studies and practises something in a single lesson today, they will probably remember at least half of the material next week.
- Once something has been learnt, further practice won't make any difference.
- Memory works like a video camera, accurately recording the events we see and hear so we can review and inspect them later.
- Some memories are stored away unconsciously but can be retrieved via hypnosis.
- In some rare cases people experience memory loss (amnesia) which causes them to forget who they are or what their name is.

A number of research studies have used statements like the ones in the box above to survey the beliefs about memory of the general public. For example, Simons and Chabris (2011, 2012) carried out two such surveys; they then followed this by asking the questions to researchers at a conference on human cognition – experts in memory, in other words. The results suggested the general public are highly inaccurate in their beliefs. For example, 63 per cent of members of the public questioned endorsed the statement above about memory working like a video camera; 0 per cent of memory researchers agreed – not a single one!

It's perhaps not surprising the general public and memory experts differ. After all, there are lots of areas where ordinary people believe things which are not true, from conspiracy theories to paranormal beliefs. Even something as common as a phobia could be seen as a false belief (i.e., believing that the object of the phobia is more dangerous than it actually is).

People are, in general, quite prone to errors in their thinking. Research by Tversky and Kahneman (1974) showed how human thinking can be biased in a number of ways. For example, the availability heuristic is where people think something is more common or probable simply because it's easier to think of an example.

We would suggest that memory and, by extension, learning are especially tricky to understand for four main reasons:

1. first, you can't *observe* encoding, storage and retrieval as they happen. You can only observe the behavioural outcome of these – such as being able to answer a question (or not). We can't look 'under the bonnet' to see what is going on when the memory is active – even in our own memories;
2. second, feedback on LTM is very slow; this is important to be aware of as a teacher and a student. With other skills, such as learning to throw a dart or paint a picture, you can get accurate and rapid feedback on your performance. You can immediately see where you went wrong. With memory and study skills, you only find out much later if your efforts were ineffective;
3. third, there are several factors which affect LTM besides a person's own immediate actions and study behaviours, and these are quite obscure to learners. For example, retaining information on a course of study doesn't depend only on the student's own approach to studying and practice. It depends on their prior knowledge of the subject, and on the type and difficulty of the material. These are things that most learners find hard to judge;
4. finally, when you have learnt things once, you can't delete the information and re-learn it using a different strategy. This makes it very hard for students to accurately compare two or more strategies.

The idea that memory is hard for students and teachers to understand is supported by the popularity of learning myths (*neuromyths*) – views of how learning works which have no real grounding in scientific evidence (Howard-Jones, 2014). They include:

- a belief that some learners are 'left brained' and others are 'right brained';
- a belief that learners have specific 'learning styles';
- a belief that we only use 10 per cent of our brains;
- a belief that learners must drink at least two litres of water per day.

Despite being flawed and unscientific, these ideas are widespread among the teaching profession worldwide, with endorsement between 58 per cent and 97 per cent for the learning styles myth among educators, and no sign of it declining (Newton & Salvi, 2020). The endorsement of such ideas suggests many educators are unsure about how learning actually works.

What's more, there appears to be no correlation between belief in neuromyths and a teacher's classroom experience, with experienced educators *less* likely to endorse evidence-based strategies (Halamish, 2018; Morehead et al., 2016). This fact supports the idea that memory is especially counterintuitive, and hard to reflect on.

## CONCLUSION

Memory is a system that is not exactly the same as learning, but underpins it. Educators can greatly benefit from understanding its key stores and processes. In this chapter, we have explored the fundamentals of working memory and long-term memory, and the idea that the goal of learning is to ensure that information enters long-term memory and remains accessible there for future use.

This involves a process of encoding, storage and retrieval. We have seen that (unlike saving files to a computer), this is not a one-off process. Forgetting occurs rapidly after a lesson, and strategies such as retrieval practice are important to making material less likely to be forgotten. It is also important to consider that while working memory can retain meaningless information, long-term retention depends on structuring what we know into meaningful schemas.

Memory is a particularly counterintuitive concept. The various misconceptions about memory and learning can be linked to the fact it is hard to be aware of what your memory is doing at any given time. We can't expect teachers, or students, to become experts in how memory works by trial and error.

## KEY POINTS

- Learning is often seen as being different from memory, but it is underpinned by memory processes.
- Although we often talk about remembering 'information', memory applies to both knowledge and skills.
- Memory comprises of working memory and long-term memory.
- Meaningful understanding is especially important to LTM.
- The 'forgetting curve' shows how forgetting is rapid at first and then slows down.
- Memory can be described in terms of a process that includes encoding, storage and retrieval.
- Storage in memory is not like that which is in a computer, and instead benefits from effective consolidation via active learning.
- Information in memory is not like a filing cabinet or computer hard drive. New memories are linked to existing knowledge and stored in structures called schemas. These schemas then affect later learning.
- There are a number of misconceptions about memory that are widespread among the general public, and probably among teachers and students too.
- Evidence on learning myths suggests memory is particularly counterintuitive, and we can't figure out how it works through classroom experience alone.

# 2

# WORKING MEMORY AND COGNITION

## INTRODUCTION

In the previous chapter, we explored the fundamental features of memory. Now, it's time to delve more deeply into the theories and supporting evidence, in order to better understand specific aspects of memory which may make a difference to student outcomes. We will begin with working memory, the system which plays a crucial role not only in retaining things over the short term, but also in processes like attention and self-regulation. What exactly is happening in a student's memory when they listen to instructions or complete a problem as part of their studies? That will be the focus on this chapter.

## THE REALM OF WORKING MEMORY

Working memory (WM) is a system for briefly retaining and processing information over a short-lived moment in time. It is a very limited memory store. It can very briefly store information that students hear, see or read, but unless they take further action, this will be lost. Knowing that facts and pieces of information we have picked up during the day do not stay in WM for more than a few seconds will help us to support learners and to plan more effective lessons.

## SCENARIO 2.1

Dr P has spent her evening carefully planning a business studies lesson where the aim is to teach students how to do cash flow forecasting. The lesson begins well, but very rapidly Dr P notices that some students are not paying attention to their work. They are getting distracted with low-level chatter, or otherwise finding it hard to focus on the task. She sees other learners not managing their time well, or leaving sections of the cash flow forecast worksheet incomplete. When Dr P circles the room and questions pupils, she realises that, despite her careful explanation and instructions, the majority of the class have forgotten certain key facts mere minutes later. Dr P feels disappointed, and realises that the lesson could have gone better.

The example in Scenario 2.1 illustrates the importance of working memory to the success of the lesson and to learning more broadly. It is a brief and unreliable store and, even when students can follow a verbal explanation, information fades very rapidly. It is also limited in its capacity. Providing both factual information and instructions verbally, even if pitched at a suitable level for a class, risks information overload.

You might be wondering what the difference is between WM and 'short-term memory'. The second of these terms was widely used in psychology research during the 1960s and 1970s. The focus was mainly on temporary storage system: using your memory to briefly retain something and repeat it back. For example, reading a postcode and then writing it down onto an envelope was seen as a typical function of short-term memory.

However, we also know that WM is involved in manipulating and processing information, such as when students do mental maths. For this reason, the modern view is to emphasise not just storage but also processing (e.g., Baddeley, 2000). Briefly retaining a small set of information is just one function of WM. So, while the two terms are sometimes used interchangeably, it seems to us that there is an important difference between the two, and for the most part we will use the broader term.

Another area of confusion here is that your students (and perhaps colleagues too) may use one or both of these terms to refer to things that are relatively long term, such as cramming for a test one evening, and then recalling what has been studied the next day. This strategy of cramming for recall, followed by a retrieval activity soon afterwards is, in fact, more a case of using LTM badly, rather than using WM. Any situation where information is held for more than a few minutes must depend on LTM, and not on WM alone.

# THE LIMITS OF WORKING MEMORY

The points and examples so far lead us to ask the question: exactly how limited is working memory? When does WM stop and LTM begin? Research has provided some tentative answers to this question:

- learners can retain a list of between five and nine random words or numbers. This is often simplified to an average of seven (the 'magical number seven', plus or minus two, as Miller, 1956, put it);
- learners can only hold four items or fewer if the items are more complex;
- our capacity for visual items is in some respects quite large, we can take in an entire visual scene in a fraction of a second. However, it is a much harder to retain and process this. When it comes to remembering a specific sequence of shapes and positions, Farrell Pagulayan et al. (2006) concluded that visual working memory is limited to around seven items in teenagers and young adults; there are no gender differences;
- the duration of working memory is very brief; items can be forgotten within a few seconds, and it is widely agreed that information will be lost from working memory in around 30 seconds or less, unless the individual does something to prevent this.

As usual, there are various caveats. Capacity also depends on the individual. Prior knowledge can help with remembering lists, but, at this point, students are not using just their working memory but borrowing from LTM as well.

## ACTIVITY

It is quite easy to test your own working memory, or that of your students. Simply prepare several lists of random numbers, random letters, or random words. Now, pair students up and have them read the lists to each other. The partner should try to repeat the items back accurately and in the right order. Start with a short list (perhaps three or four items) and gradually increase the number. At what point does accuracy (in terms of getting the entire list correct and in the right order) drop below 50 per cent?

A visual version of this is known as the Corsi test – you can find versions online. It involves remembering a sequence of dots or shapes on a screen. You could also experiment with using a meaningful paragraph, rather than random words. What difference does this make?

Overall, it may be useful to think of WM as a workspace – the mental equivalent of the surface of your desk. As it is small in size, learners can only work on a bit of new information at time. The limitations of WM therefore point to certain ways that students can struggle in the classroom. Table 2.1, below, gives some examples of these situations, and highlights possible solutions:

**Table 2.1**    Examples of working memory

| Problem | What might this look like in the classroom? | Subsequent result on working memory | Solution |
|---|---|---|---|
| Too much information | A teacher is dictating a text to a group of learners in a religious studies lesson about the large number of steps taken in the Islamic Prayer. | If learners are given lots of different information to process at the one time, they may struggle to cope with it. Students can only process a certain number of words at a time. | Break down the teaching of concepts into one or two smaller 'chunks', and stop to check pupil understanding before moving on. |
| Distracting information | When an A-level psychology teacher is introducing the concept of attachment of a child to their caregiver, he adds an unrelated anecdote about his own parents. | Related to the capacity limits of WM, people may forget things if additional, distracting information is shared at the same time as the target information. | Plan carefully how concepts will be introduced during the lesson to students. Be wary of adding extra information as it occurs to you. |
| Too much complexity | A science teacher is trying to explain how vaccines are created and used around the world. They introduce lots of complex concepts and examples, rapidly getting into some very technical explanations. | If students are grappling with novel or complex concepts, this will be much more difficult than holding simpler sets of information. | Write the information down chronologically. Consider presenting it in smaller chunks, and combine the use of images with text (e.g., a flow chart) to make new information easier to process. |
| Time constraints | A new teacher is trying to learn the names of the students who they only see for an hour once a week. | Students' names will fade very fast from the teacher's WM, in a matter of seconds or minutes, making them hard to memorise. | Make use of retrieval practice by saying student names throughout the lesson, e.g., 'Hamid did you want to ask a question ...?'; 'Owami, please share your example on the board.' |

# THE ROLE OF MEANING

As mentioned in Chapter 1, WM is not especially sensitive to meaning; we can briefly retain a random string of words and numbers, and repeat them back or note then down. However, we also know that a student integrating new knowledge with their schemas is an important part of learning. This is part of what working memory does when a student completes a task.

Consider the following sentences (based on Bransford & Stein, 1993):

- John walked on the roof.
- Bill picked up the egg.

It would be hard for students to retain the information; the names would quickly fade from WM. But what about the following alternatives?

- Santa Claus walked on the roof.
- The Easter Bunny picked up the egg.

Here, learners can use WM to integrate their existing knowledge with the new information. The sentences might be new to them, but they can make sense of them, and doing so will lead to the information being better remembered.

Overall, these points show that while working memory is not a system that focuses on meaning, it interacts closely with meaning-based LTM. While the limits of WM should be considered when planning classroom activities, we certainly should not ignore the vital importance of prior knowledge or meaningful understanding.

# ATTENTION AND AUTOMATICITY

You may wonder how learners manage to do such complex things if working memory can only hold a few items at a time. How, for example, does a student watch a video with complex images and words, engage in lightning-speed thinking and reactions during a sports match, or a read a book at high speed?

The answer is that some things become automatic with practice. Reading is a prime example of this. What is slow and laborious for the younger child soon becomes so fluent that their eyes don't even fixate on each word on the page.

Tasks which have become automatic demand less attention. Attention is another way in which the human mind is limited, and it plays a key role in how working memory functions. Students can only pay attention to so many things at once during a given time.

Just as WM can be a bottleneck for information entering LTM, our capacity to pay attention can also be a bottleneck for taking things into WM in the first place. A lot of things are happening at once in the classroom or other learning environments, and learners need to select the right things and pay attention to them (words, numbers, images or other information) in order for these things to enter WM. They then need to continue to pay attention in order to maintain this information in WM, and to problem solve or manipulate ideas in their mind. However, things that are partially or entirely automatic take up little or no attention, freeing working memory up to focus on other things.

Many of the things we associate with poor memory among students (failing to retain instructions, for example) may in fact be more to do with insufficient attention being paid. Often these are non-routine tasks which cannot become automatic because they are different every time – remembering this week's homework, for example.

Attention is more limited than learners themselves tend to realise. Students often believe they can multitask effectively. In part this is because they *can* do some tasks fairly automatically, such as copying a text or repeating a list of words. However, if a student is not giving a task their full attention, their ability to use the information or to link it to existing schemas will be very limited.

Consider the following examples:

## SCENARIO 2.2

When Sally first started learning to drive, she had to remember to coordinate the steering wheel, press the clutch and change gear all at the same time. This was difficult, and she sometimes didn't get the sequence correct, sometimes leading the car to stall. Over time, and with practice, Sally can now change the gears in her car and control the steering wheel while having a conversation with the person in the car. These actions have become automatic for her.

In a computing science lesson, students have been learning to code a series of simple puzzle games. Initially, writing code is challenging. For many learners, their programs do not run as intended and stop part-way through. Over the school year, the students get faster at writing code and spot errors more quickly.

Mohammed is trying to revise for a test in French that he has the following morning. Mohammed also wants to watch a football match and tries to do both things at the same time. Later, he finds that he gets some of the French phrases mixed up, and struggles to remember what he has practised.

The examples in Scenario 2.2 shows how valuable automaticity is. Because Sally's attention is limited, it is really useful to do basic driving tasks automatically. This frees up attention to focus on other things. And as with the computing students, even things like spotting errors can become more automatic, while processes such as writing or coding become more fluent.

The example of Mohammed shows that we shouldn't assume that every task can be done automatically. Most homework and study tasks will be highly demanding of attention, and can't be completed automatically alongside another task. This is why it's such a bad idea for learners to multitask while studying (background music may be less problematic – if students are coping well when studying with background music and find it motivating to do so, it's probably not worth trying to stop them!).

Of course, as every teacher knows, learners don't always pay attention to the right things. If learners are distracted, for example by something that is happening outside the classroom window, their limited attention simply cannot cope. Younger students in particular are poor at managing their own attention, and it is to be expected that this self-regulation skill will take a lot of time to master.

## MIND-WANDERING

Closely related to the idea of distractions, *mind-wandering* is where learners' attention is focused internally on their own thoughts, rather than on their work or something in the classroom. This is a problem when a teacher is explaining something or otherwise providing new information. A lack of attention to the task at hand means that information is not being processed and therefore won't enter LTM.

### SCENARIO 2.3

Miss Klee has asked students to create a pencil sketch of their favourite animal. Miss Klee quickly notices that the students who find drawing enjoyable are concentrating well and making good progress. However, she is concerned to notice that a few students have started to wander round the room to sharpen pencils, chatting about things not related to the task. Others are sitting at their desk, staring into space and not drawing. A few have still not started the task, despite Miss Klee prompting them. Miss Klee decides to sanction the students that are not currently drawing.

The example in Scenario 2.3 shows how easy it is for pupils' attention to wander. Many teachers would agree that pupils who are off task should be sanctioned in some way. However, there are a couple of aspects to consider before we condemn mind-wandering as a 'bad thing':

- it's inevitable. Everyone mind-wanders every single day. We can't stop our students from doing it, so it may be more realistic to manage and account for it when planning;
- in some situations, mind-wandering appears to be helpful for problem solving and creativity. When mind-wandering, learners may be making connections between new information and concepts and existing knowledge.

Given these facts, educators shouldn't attempt to ban mind-wandering, or punish students for doing it. We should instead make allowances for it, and even encourage it at certain times – for example, by prompting students to engage in quiet contemplation for creative tasks. In Scenario 2.3, Miss Klee should probably intervene when pupils are walking about and chatting, but the pupils who are at their desk and thinking may just need more time to come up with ideas.

## SCENARIO 2.4

In a personal development lesson, students are asked to consider arguments for and against the government extending the mandatory hours spent on physical exercise in school. Instructions are displayed on a whiteboard and also stated verbally. Students then engage in a group discussion. At this point, some group members appear quiet and disengaged for a while, lost in thought.

The example in Scenario 2.4 shows how mind-wandering might occur in the classroom. It may look to the teacher and other group members as if the quiet students have lost their focus. However, it is possible that they are merely thinking through the issues as part of what is a complex task. If so, this could be a beneficial use of their time. In future, when planning, the teacher may build in some thinking time, perhaps combined with individual note-taking.

## COGNITIVE LOAD

A term which is closely related to WM and increasingly widespread in education over recent years is 'cognitive load'. This means the burden placed on a person's mind when they engage in cognitive processes. In other words, cognitive load is the demand placed on the learner's working memory at any given time.

We should be aware that cognitive load can vary a lot for each individual student in the class, depending on such factors as the task a student is doing at that time, or their prior knowledge (see 'The Role of Meaning', above).

Many people in education feel that teachers should pay more attention to cognitive load, taking the limits of working memory into account when designing tasks and programmes of instruction (Shibli & West, 2018). It is also recognised that when learners have well-organised schemas, this can help them to manage cognitive load, aiding their learning.

There is evidence that prior knowledge can affect the capacity of WM, and it makes *cognitive sense* that processing space could to some extent be freed up by automaticity of prior knowledge. For example, knowing basic facts about atoms from the periodic table reduces load on working memory when doing a chemistry calculation, compared to having to stop and struggle to remember these, or look them up.

Overall, the idea of managing cognitive load makes sense for three main reasons:

- first, it is generally agreed that WM is strictly limited in its capacity; it is therefore possible for any learner's WM to be overloaded;
- second, the amount of time that WM can hold information for is limited;
- finally, if the limits of WM are exceeded in terms of either its capacity (too much information causes some of it to be pushed out of the WM) or duration (information is forgotten because too much time has passed), this will affect a student's ability to encode that information to the LTM.

However, working memory has both a verbal and a visual store, and this creates some questions which need exploring further. If the verbal store is overloaded, could a learner use their visual store instead? Is it possible that they could use notes or diagrams to offload some of the processing? How do these constraints play out in more self-regulated learning situations, such as independent study, when a learner could slow down and take their time over a complex task? What role, if any, does extraneous information play?

To explore these questions, it makes sense to establish a slightly more detailed model of working memory for you to think about as you proceed with this chapter. We turn to this next.

## THEORIES OF WORKING MEMORY

While issues such as the limits of WM or the effect of automaticity have broad research support, there is not currently a single, universally agreed theory of working memory. We will therefore introduce three broad perspectives of working memory, comment on each one, and try to come to some kind of resolution that highlights the most important issues that teachers might need to think about.

## WORKING MEMORY AS A UNITARY STORE

This view, exemplified by the theories of Atkinson and Shiffrin (1968) or the work of Sweller and colleagues (e.g., Sweller, 1990), is the simplest of the models and sees working memory as a limited box which holds information for a brief period of time. Information enters this box via the senses. Once information enters WM, three things can happen to it:

1. information can be rehearsed, meaning that we are doing something with it to keep it active;
2. it can be forgotten;
3. it can be encoded to long-term memory.

The benefits of keeping things active in working memory are that they aren't forgotten in the here and now, prior to the point at which the learner wants to use the information. This is straightforward to understand. For example, you may need to retain a particular number in your head until you are ready to do the next step of a calculation in maths or science.

Likewise, if you want to retain a short list of items that you need to buy, such as 'a loaf of bread, a container of milk and a stick of butter', you can probably see how repeating those over and over could help them to stay 'active' in working memory. If someone was to say these things all the way to the shops, it would help them to maintain the items in WM and not forget them. Psychologists call this process *maintenance rehearsal*.

It also seems clear and logical that the other two main options are that the information is successfully transferred to LTM or forgotten entirely. In fact, some researchers believe that keeping things active in WM (option 1, above) is the main way of *encoding* them to LTM (option 3, above). However, there are some problems with the idea that getting things into LTM is just a matter of repeating them, an idea that links to strategies such as drilling, re-reading and rote rehearsal in the classroom. We will explore this issue further in Chapter 3.

Overall, this model is easy for teachers to grasp, but it also lacks some important details. Viewing WM as a general-purpose box does not really tell us much about the different types of information that can be held in working memory. As mentioned earlier, we can hold and process both auditory information and visual imagery, as well as text, emotions and information from the other senses. What's more, there are clear differences in terms of how these are processed in WM. For example, it is much easier to engage in maintenance rehearsal of the number bonds from the times tables than to mentally rehearse an image or diagram from your notes.

The second limitation is that this perspective sees processing in WM as separate from LTM. In fact, the processing we do – reading a book, for example – is supported by our background knowledge from our LTM (as discussed earlier). Someone with a lot of knowledge of working memory could read and take in the arguments from this chapter faster than someone who is new to the concept. It's not because the novice has a weaker or smaller working memory, but rather because of less well-developed schemas in LTM.

These problems are tackled, at least to an extent, in the following two alternative views of WM.

## WORKING MEMORY AS A MULTI-PART STORE

An obvious way to tackle the over-simplistic ideas discussed above is to expand on them with more detail. Working memory as a multi-part store is often presented as a more detailed version of the unitary store. Rather than presenting working memory as a single box that holds information temporarily, it 'zooms in' and shows that working memory itself has multiple parts.

This is exactly the approach that several researchers have taken. The best-known and most influential example is Baddeley's (2000) theory of working memory, and we will focus on this for the remainder of this section. This theory includes:

- a two-part verbal system for words and sounds that includes both a store and a maintenance rehearsal system. In the classroom, this would be involved when students answer questions, read a piece of text 'in their head', or listen to other students;
- a visual store for visual and spatial information. In the classroom, this would be involved when students process images from a slide, look at displays on the classroom walls, compare two images, or construct mind maps;
- the *episodic buffer*, a store that helps an individual connect together information from the different senses into single a coherent experience. In the classroom, this

would be involved when students take in both visual information from a slide and a teacher's verbal explanation, and form a coherent memory of the experience that they could later discuss.

All three of these stores are assumed to connect to the different parts of LTM (Baddeley, 2000), but are also able to function and process independently. In addition, a fourth major part of the model called the *central executive* is responsible for controlling each store, and allocates attention to specific tasks.

There are several classroom implications of this model:

*   the fact that WM is seen as having both a verbal and visual store puts the emphasis more on attention. Learners can hold both verbal and visual information in mind at the same time, as long as neither is especially complex. For example, in the classroom this might be when we are teaching using PowerPoint slides and present some visual diagrams alongside the text;
*   each store has its own limits, but learners can use capacity in one to help out. For example, if verbal information is too complex, a learner can use images to help them remember. Perhaps students in a biology lesson are reading a text about photosynthesis with a diagram alongside. If they struggle to make sense of the text alone, they can use the diagram to support their understanding;
*   rather than seeing the limits of WM as holding approximately seven items in a single store, this model sees the limitation as based around the amount of time that it would take to say verbal information. This shows the value of giving students a little more time on a task, especially if they are struggling;
*   the central executive helps learners to keep themselves on track, while the other stores do more basic processing. It is vital for self-regulation and metacognition.

## ACTIVITY

Try rehearsing the following lists of words by reading them and then writing them on a separate page. Do this for the list of short words first, then for the list of long words. You will find you retain the short words more readily in the working memory than the long words. This demonstrates that the amount of time it would take to say verbal information is a key limit, not just the number of items.

*(Continued)*

| Short words | Long words |
| --- | --- |
| Raft | Refrigerator |
| Feed | Association |
| Slow | Imagination |
| Gate | Opportunity |
| Month | University |
| Lawn | Geographical |
| Main | Considerable |
| Wit | Intimidating |

Although the idea of working memory as a multi-part store makes things a bit more complex, it allows for more precision. Other models of memory have divided up working memory in slightly different ways, but the overall principle of multiple stores that can work independently is common to all such models.

However, a limitation of multi-component views of WM is that they still see processing as largely separate from LTM. Often, supporting research is conducted using meaningless lists of words, helping to keep LTM out of the picture as far as possible.

In everyday life, things are a bit more complicated. The functioning of WM is strongly linked to LTM and in the classroom we use both simultaneously. As such, it could be argued that tasks which isolate WM and focus on it alone are so exceptional that they aren't very informative about what happens in the classroom. The next view of working memory seeks to place more emphasis on how WM works *together* with LTM.

## INTEGRATED VIEW OF MEMORY

An alternative view of working memory focuses on the way WM and LTM interact. This *integrated view* involves focusing on the way that WM links with and is supported by LTM, and avoids trying to artificially separate the two. A major example is the research of Ericsson and Kintsch (1995).

When we take this perspective, we begin to observe some memory features that could be important in the classroom. For example, even the limits of WM can be overcome when LTM starts to play its part. As discussed earlier in this chapter, a standard idea is that WM can only hold around seven verbal items, and when it comes to attention and processing, the limit is closer to four. However, if students read a meaningful passage of text, they can typically remember more meaningful concepts than that, due to support from LTM. What's more, working memory is considerably less limited in areas where the learner has some expertise (Ericsson & Kintsch, 1995).

Although this is perhaps less neat than the first two models presented, it is a bit more realistic. There are plenty of educational tasks where long-term memories and knowledge affect processing. In reading, for example, the actions of working memory are guided by long-term knowledge. Readers can scan over sections that already seem familiar, and stop and repeat things – thinking about the words on the page and accessing schemas – if they struggle to understand a particular sentence or passage. Trying to understand working memory in isolation can therefore be seen as unrealistic from a classroom perspective. It never operates alone.

Likewise, the way that we use attention to guide and select among tasks – a function of the central executive as described in Baddeley's multi-component model – could also be guided by prior knowledge from LTM. This will especially play a role when experienced learners decide what to focus on, or use their experience to ignore distractions.

## CONCLUSION

In this chapter, we have explored the important role that working memory can play in the classroom. As a cognitive system which stores and processes information, it is involved in virtually every educational task and activity. It is also very limited, both in its capacity and in terms of how long things can be held.

The limits of working memory have implications for how much information we should present to students. However, the situation does get easier as knowledge and skills become learnt to the point that they are largely automatic. This means that less attention needs to be paid to the basic nuts and bolts of a task, allowing learners to focus on other things such as the strategy to solve a problem.

The limits on working memory are sometimes seen in terms of cognitive load, but this is based on a rather simplistic model of working memory, which doesn't account for different sub-systems. More recent models account for learners having separate verbal and visual stores in WM, and place more emphasis on how working memory and LTM connect and interact.

# KEY POINTS

- Working memory has certain key limitations to its capacity and in terms of how long it can hold information.
- Working memory depends on attention, which is also limited. However, attention can be freed up when tasks become more automatic. The attention-based system is sometimes called the central executive, and it plays a role in self-regulation.
- The view of working memory as a unitary store is convenient but limited. There is broad agreement that working memory has both a verbal and a visual store. If the verbal store is overloaded, a learner may be able to use their visual store instead or as well.
- While much research into working memory seeks to isolate it, in real educational situations it combines closely with LTM. LTM can guide and inform processes like reading and creativity, and allow learners to overcome some of the limits of working memory.

# 3

# LONG-TERM MEMORY: THE BASICS

## INTRODUCTION

In the first chapter of this book, we introduced you to some of the main features of long-term memory (LTM). We will now explore how LTM works and the theory behind it, and clarify certain key principles that can be applied to all aspects of learning across the curriculum. Most importantly of all, we will explore how students can store things in LTM memory in way which will be resilient, well organised and retrievable.

A key question that you might have about LTM is around how long it lasts. How long is 'long'? We know that working memory is a very brief memory store; LTM comes into play for any information which we want to store beyond the current task. Even storing something for a few minutes while you work on another task would be considered a function of long-term rather than working memory.

LTM can therefore be seen as a permanent storage system, or at least one that *supports* permanent storage. How well things are actually accessible later on depends on a number of important factors which are important for teachers to understand. These will be explored in this chapter.

It is worth bearing in mind that LTM will be at work even when it is not being used effectively – for example, when students cram for tests and exams. These students are using LTM; it's just that they are not using it effectively. Perhaps rather than focusing on its 'long' duration, it is more useful to see LTM as the memory store which holds information while you are doing something else. If your students can retain something without paying attention to it – for example, while distracted by a conversation, or overnight – then we can say that LTM is at work.

All the same, we need to be aware LTM is subject to forgetting. It is a misconception to see our memories as a permanent recording and, of course, students who use flawed study strategies often cannot recall the bulk of what they have tried to memorise. You could consider the task of retrieving memories as being rather like finding something in a messy cupboard in your home. It might be in there, but you can't necessarily locate it when needed.

New knowledge and skills need to be stored permanently, but they also need to be *accessible*, so learners can retrieve them when needed. This includes applying what they have learnt in a new context or unfamiliar situation, when undertaking further study, or in the workplace.

## THE BASIC OUTLINE OF LTM

Trying to sketch a basic outline of what LTM looks like in practice has proved even harder for researchers to do than is the case with working memory. There are multiple theories, and each focuses on particular aspects without necessarily capturing LTM as a whole system.

Perhaps the most widely used model is the idea that LTM is a simple storage system or 'box', to which working memory is connected and acts as a gateway. Together with the simple model of working memory shown in Chapter 2, this forms Atkinson and Shiffrin's (1968) 'multi-store' model of memory.

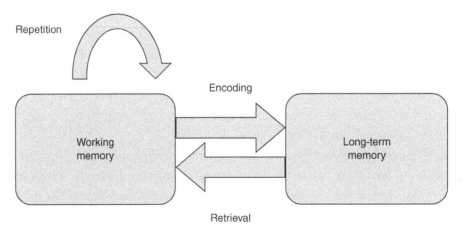

**Figure 3.1**   Multi-store model

The multi-store model suggests that WM and LTM connect together, and that they each work in fundamentally different ways. This idea is accepted by most memory researchers.

A key claim made by this model is that information needs to be processed in working memory in order to enter LTM, and the extent and duration of this processing correlates with how efficiently encoding happens. This idea is reflected in the following quote: 'Memory is the residue of thought' (Willingham, 2009). That is to say, the more we think about and process something in working memory, the more likely it is to be encoded to LTM.

The model does not illuminate what memories actually *do* once they are in LTM, or account for a memory being modified or edited after it is stored, something that happens often in education when learners are asked to reconsider or elaborate on information. It also does not tell us anything about how memories connect together. As discussed previously, memories cluster into networks called schemas (see Chapter 1), and this is important when students make connections across different school subjects.

Some of the main things this model fails to account for include:

- the fact that practice alone doesn't ensure memorisation;
- the role of active learning;
- the role of schemas, or previous learning already held in the LTM;
- the fact the content of LTM (or the knowledge and skills) influences processing in working memory;
- the fact some items (for example, stimuli which are dangerous or are personal to the learner) are more memorable than others;
- storage of different types of information (for example, verbal, visual).

These are significant omissions! As educators, we cannot ignore such major factors, as they affect whether curriculum-relevant material will be remembered or forgotten by our students.

The multi-store model is what theorists would describe as an information-processing model; LTM is compared to the storage of a computer. Many of the factors in the bullet points above don't apply to computer storage, but they *do* apply to real-world human learning. If anything, this just serves to remind us that computer analogies are limited. Like any analogy, this one has the potential to illuminate, but also the potential to mislead.

## ACTIVITY

Try the following activity. Look at the following list of words for ten to twenty seconds, then cover the page and write down everything you can remember.

| | |
|---|---|
| Sharp | Syringe |
| Injection | Thread |
| Haystack | Knitting |
| Straw | Sewing. |

The task you just tried is known as the Deese–Roediger–McDermott paradigm. Did you include the word 'needle' in your response? It's not there in the list! A great many experimental participants tend to include it. This demonstration shows the contents of LTM – in this case, the meaningful connections between words – can affect performance on a WM task.

In the classroom, the same phenomenon could occur when reading a story in English. As they read, the learners are making sense of the story using associations with existing knowledge to help them follow and understand it. The significance of the hand washing in the plot of *Macbeth*, for example, requires each learner to access schemas around guilt and contamination. This shows that long-term memories don't just sit passively in a box while students rehearse new things in working memory. Rather, memories form a network, and previously learnt information in LTM affects how learners understand incoming material.

## THE ROLE OF FORGETTING AND SPACING

We will explore the multi-store model and address the 'gaps' in the model one at a time in order to get a fuller picture of how LTM operates in the classroom. However, first let's explore the role of spacing and decay of memories over time, which the model partially addresses.

LTM is subject to forgetting and this proceeds according to the forgetting curve (see Chapter 1), so students forget their learning fast at first, and later slower.

We call this forgetting process in LTM *decay*, meaning as time passes things start to disappear.

The concept of decay is included within the multi-store model, and fits with the need for consolidation of learning over time – something every teacher recognises as critical. As memories are forgotten, the model implies re-learning after a delay would be more beneficial than doing it straight away.

## SCENARIO 3.1

Mrs T teaches her class about how to work out coordinates on a map in her geography lesson. She then sets an activity a few lessons later asking students to come in and start the task on their desk. The task is to identify and mark coordinates on a worksheet using the learning they did in their previous lesson. Mrs T finds some of the students have forgotten how to use coordinates. This skill needs to be refreshed in order for them to progress with the task.

The idea of delayed practice fits with the spacing effect, in other words, that learning is better remembered if practice is delayed. As Bjork and Bjork (2011) explain, it would be better for a learner to wait until they were on the verge of forgetting something before practising it again. Practice which is scheduled to happen after some forgetting has taken place – as in the example with Mrs T and her lesson on map coordinates in Scenario 3.1 – helps to secure new learning. And as time goes on, forgetting slows and retrieving the information again becomes easier and more automatic.

In the classroom, learners can be reminded of ideas just as those ideas are beginning to fade, and may remember things partially, or with errors. However, the multi-store model sees information as being 100 per cent present or absent in LTM, and has no way of explaining things being *weakly* present, or *partially* present. The modal model also doesn't provide any useful guidance on the timing of classroom practice at all.

Perhaps most importantly, we shouldn't see learning new material as being a one-off event. Instead, delayed consolidation is necessary to gradually boost the storage strength of a memory (see also 'A Developed Theory', below).

When making use of the spacing effect:

- learners will master something via an initial study session – in Mrs T's lesson above this was learning how to add coordinates to a map;
- learners will return to the material and practise it actively after a delay – in Mrs T's lesson this was a starter activity a few weeks after the initial learning;
- learners will revisit the material again on at least one occasion, with the practice now becoming more complex and interlinked with other material. In Mrs T's lesson students may learn to change incorrect coordinates on a map. With further practice and through linking in other knowledge, they will be able to explain the impact of inaccurate coordinates – for example, when the emergency services are attempting to locate someone for mountain rescue.

## REFLECTION POINT

It is widely considered the spacing effect should be applied more widely in schools. How exactly would this work in your context?

## ACTIVITY

Try to think of a specific way you could change the timing of practice for learners in your context. For example, is there a consolidation task or test which could take place after a delay of at least a week? Could a project task encompass meaningful review and consolidation of a previous topic?

Remember, using the spacing effect well means learners should get a chance to study something in enough depth to grasp it on the first occasion. Then there should be enough of a time delay that they are on the verge of forgetting before they next practice. How long that delay should be depends on a number of factors, including the learners and the type of material being studied.

## PRACTICE ALONE DOESN'T ENSURE MEMORISATION

The multi-store model emphasises the processes of repetition and maintenance of ideas in working memory as the key route into LTM; the 'residue of thought' idea. If we think about and practise things a lot, it implies, then they should stick in our memory.

However, we also know that learners can think about things *a lot* and still fail to remember them. Most teachers have experienced the situation where ideas and skills that were practised intensively as part of previous lessons are apparently absent at the time of an assessment. Likewise, things we could do with ease when we ourselves were at school are not always remembered easily now. Could you get the same grades on your school exams if you sat the papers today? Sadly, it's not uncommon for learners to retain very little of the information and skills covered in a school course, especially if they are tested months or years later.

It is not the amount of study time that matters but how *effective* the methods used during a study session are. Consider, for example, the issue of 'retrieval practice vs re-reading', which has already been discussed. These might take a similar amount of time, but retrieval practice is more effective. Clearly, just holding information in your working memory is not the whole story. It matters what you *do* with that information. Further evidence comes from research on homework by Schumann et al. (1985). They found that hours spent studying homework account for less than 1 per cent of the variance in students' grades.

This means that putting in the hours is a very limited strategy. It's much more important that the hours are being used effectively. Naturally, this is great news for students! They can study for *less* time and get *better* results.

## THE ROLE OF ACTIVE LEARNING

A further fundamental limitation of the multi-store model is that it does not account for active learning. Although repetition in working memory is to some extent an active task, we have probably all been in the situation where we repeat a phrase without really focusing our attention on it. For example, you can probably do an everyday task while repeatedly muttering, 'one, two, three; one, two, three ...' under your breath.

Likewise, a learner can listen to a lecture or read something on a whiteboard and screen – and perhaps even copy it into their notes – without really taking it in. It's unlikely that they will remember much of what they wrote down, if anything, when doing this task in a way that requires neither paying full attention to the content, nor actively doing anything with the information.

This is why *active learning* is seen as important. Our definition of this term does not imply that learners need to be physically active. However, they do need to *do* something with the material. Active learning implies that they are using information, thinking about it and processing it in some way, rather than passively listening, re-reading, or copying. So, when planning for learning, it is important to consider what the students will do with the material. Teaching it in small chunks of learning with time to practise built in (as recommended by Rosenshine, 2012) helps to ensure the learning is active.

## A DEVELOPED THEORY

We have seen that the multi-store model presents a useful outline, but omits some important details. The *new theory of disuse* is another major theory of LTM and, in our view, a more practically useful one. It will inform the next few sections.

Developed by Robert Bjork and colleagues, the new theory of disuse doesn't look at LTM as a box where things are passively stored and gradually forgotten, but rather sees each memory as having a chance of being retrieved that depends on what we do with it. This is much more applicable to teaching and learning in the classroom. It also places much less emphasis on short-term repetition (quite the opposite, in fact).

### STORAGE STRENGTH VS RETRIEVAL STRENGTH

The theory distinguishes between two properties any memory has – storage strength and retrieval strength. Any educational experience or task can affect the chance that a memory is more easily retrieved in future and can affect how securely it is stored. It doesn't necessarily affect both things equally.

Storage and retrieval of memory might sound similar, but we have already looked at how they can be seen as two separate processes in memory (see Chapter 1). In the context of the new theory of disuse, storage and retrieval strength again have a fundamental difference between them:

- retrieval strength relates to how easily we can bring something to mind and therefore affects *performance* in the here and now, or in the near future;
- storage strength relates to how securely something is stored in LTM and therefore affects learning and transfer both now and over the long term.

We can, in fact, put these two things on a diagram, and consider every memory in terms of both storage and retrieval.

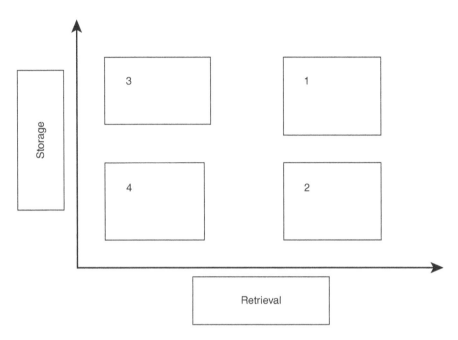

**Figure 3.2**   Retrieval strength and storage strength of memories

The best-case scenario is clearly that things are *both* easy to retrieve and securely stored (area 1 on the graph). Memories with these features spring easily to mind and can be recalled and used after a considerable delay. But what would it look like if this wasn't the case?

- If a memory has high retrieval strength but low storage strength (area 2 on the diagram), it can be recalled in the near future (hours or days) but will soon be forgotten, like material a learner has crammed the night before a test or exam.
- Typically, a person's memory for their hotel room number also has high retrieval strength but low storage strength. Most people can remember their hotel room number during a stay, even after a delay of a few hours while they are doing another task such as sightseeing. It's therefore stored in LTM, not working memory. But can you remember your hotel room numbers from last year, or five years

ago? For most people, the answer is 'no'. This temporary information fades rapidly from memory and is not well stored over the long term.

- If a memory has high storage strength but low retrieval strength (area 3), this means it is in LTM but hard to get out when needed. These are the memories which are really hard to dredge up from your mind. In education, an example might be when a student sits in an exam hall and struggles to remember something. In a more everyday context, something like the postcode of your childhood home or the names of distant relatives might have high storage strength but low retrieval strength. The information is in there, but it probably takes you some time to retrieve.

- If memories have low storage strength and low retrieval strength (area 4), this is the worst-case scenario. These have not been securely learnt, and they don't come to mind easily either. If students didn't engage in effective practice and consolidation during the lesson, then they probably couldn't tell you the key information five minutes later, never mind retrieve it months later in their exam.

## THE ROLE OF ORGANISATION

You might wonder why some information which is intensively studied, for example via cramming in the lead up to an exam, has low storage strength. At its worst, cramming leads to taking in a bunch of disconnected facts without understanding how they relate to the broader topic. The information has high retrieval strength, but only temporarily. Forgetting is already kicking in fast, before the student even gets to the exam hall. How can it be *in* LTM, and then later be gone? And why do some things stick with us, even when we weren't making much effort to learn them?

The answer relates to schemas. These are organising structures in memory (see Chapter 1). If information isn't connected together – meaningfully organised – then the learner ends up with knowledge that isn't sufficiently resilient or flexible. Additionally, the disconnected nature of the facts makes it harder for learners to *think with* the information. A learner can't make comparisons, analogies, or use the information to help them evaluate other ideas, and knowledge is harder to apply (Perkins & Salomon, 1988; Willingham, 2007). These skills (evaluation, application, etc.) are, of course, central to many courses.

We will say much more about the role of meaningful understanding in the next chapter, but it is worth pointing out that for a student to understand information and connect it into schemas makes that material more resilient, and less prone to forgetting. However, it still needs to be consolidated actively, and after a delay.

## PERFORMANCE VS LEARNING

Retrieval strength and storage strength are useful, but they remain theoretical ideas and, without more information, it is hard to know what strength a specific memory will have. Soderstrom and Bjork (2015) make the ideas of retrieval strength and storage strength more relevant to the classroom by linking them to two educational ideas we can actually observe:

- *performance*: how well and accurately a learner can do a task in the here and now. Are they fluent and able to avoid errors?
- *learning*: how well and accurately a learner can do a task after a lengthy delay or in a different context.

Good performance, on the one hand, indicates high retrieval strength. It means the learner can do the task in the here and now, and they may well leave the classroom or study session feeling confident. But this can be misleading.

Learning, on the other hand, is underpinned by high storage strength (though high retrieval strength is also very helpful). This is where information is well embedded in memory and can be retrieved and used out of context and after a delay – for example, when learners can use maths concepts years later in a science class.

A key idea the researchers raise in their paper is that performance and learning are negatively correlated. Strategies that improve performance are *worse* for learning:

- better performance in class – worse learning;
- worse performance in class – better learning.

If that sounds bizarre, take a moment to consider some real examples. The counter-intuitive idea makes sense when you reflect back on some of what you have read so far in this book.

Consider, for example, repetition versus retrieval practice. It's easier for learners to copy from a slide or textbook, or to repeat things verbatim. It's harder for them to retrieve these things actively from memory. They will make more errors on a retrieval practice task, but it is better for learning.

The spacing effect is another clear example. A delay will make performance worse, but it is a more effective way of getting things to stick.

These examples show we shouldn't seek or encourage perfect performance in the classroom. A very easy consolidation test would be like lifting a weight at the gym. If it's too easy, it is of little benefit. If pupils are making no mistakes, is it possible their tasks are too easy and don't include enough active, retrieved or delayed elements? At times, practice needs to be more challenging in order to make learning more effective.

This idea is summed up by a term that has become widely used in education over recent years – 'desirable difficulties'. A desirable difficulty is a strategy that makes tasks more difficult for students (leading to more of a struggle and probably increased errors), but in a good way (Bjork & Bjork, 2011) in that it promotes learning rather than performance. Retrieval and spacing are both desirable difficulties and, arguably, most forms of active learning are desirable difficulties too. Further examples will be discussed later in this chapter.

It's tempting as a teacher to think a key part of one's job is to make things as straightforward as possible for the learners during a task. The idea of performance vs learning helps us to reconsider this. We should be aiming to improve learning, not performance.

Another surprising point made by the researchers behind the new theory of disuse is as follows: 'Forgetting can foster learning' (Soderstrom & Bjork, 2015, p. 192). If it seems strange that forgetting would be useful, consider this – that's exactly what is happening with the spacing effect. More time passing means more forgetting is taking place. But this means that future practice is more impactful.

## REFLECTION POINT

Take a moment to think about some of the practice and consolidation tasks that you have used. Are they challenging enough? And do you emphasise and encourage perfect performance?

## ACTIVITY

Note down three or four ways in which tasks may be made less routine and challenging in your context.

## REALISM AND TRANSFER

You might be wondering *why* factors such as retrieval practice and spacing boost learning rather than performance. The researchers behind the new theory of disuse have an elegant explanation for this.

In their 2011 chapter, Robert and Elizabeth Bjork point out that a lot of the strategies which are considered evidence-based mimic real-world learning situations in some way. Consider, for example, how we learn to drive. It wouldn't be helpful to make practice very easy and repetitive, such as driving around the same block again and again. It would lead to good performance, but poor learning, as it wouldn't prepare us for the real thing.

Or think about remembering how to change a tyre or set up a spreadsheet. In the workplace or everyday life, these are not tasks you would do several times in the same day. They are things which happen occasionally, at times unpredictably, and you have to remember what to do from memory. That is to say, you need to retrieve the skills and knowledge actively, in a different context, and after a delay.

These examples show that a key consideration in memory-informed teaching is that the practice should, as far as possible, resemble the situation where knowledge and skills are later used. The difficulties which improve learning mimic real-world challenges. When students leave the classroom and use their learning in the real world, they will have to retrieve relevant skills and knowledge, use them actively and do so out of context and after a delay. These same factors make practice more effective. It means the practice was better preparation for the real thing. Thus, it's not just *any* difficulty that we want, but one which prepares the learner for later use and application of what they have learnt.

It's worth focusing in on the idea of the real-world context. Psychologists have known for decades that memories are harder to retrieve in a context which doesn't resemble the learning situation. Even Pavlov's dog responded less strongly to a tone which was higher or lower pitched. For our learners, it's vital they can recognise new contexts and apply what they have learnt. Researchers call this *transfer*.

For example, it's not very helpful if geography students are great at recognising map features in a classroom, but totally unable to recognise them when out hiking or mountain climbing. The skill needs to transfer.

As another example, consider the language skills we hope students will learn in English language classes. The intention is for these to transfer, so the learners become better at using language in their lives more broadly. But does studying a poem at age 14 really make you better at giving a workplace speech, or writing a technical manual?

Psychologists have come to recognise transfer is actually very difficult. This is well set out by researchers Barnett and Ceci (2002). They explain a system of transfer according to the following principles, each of which vary on a continuum from low to high:

- how similar is the topic/subject (for example, science vs arts)?
- how similar is the physical context (for example, a lab vs outdoors)?
- how similar is the stimulus (for example, transferring facts about a bird's biology to a reptile vs to a worm)?
- how recently did the initial learning take place (for example, yesterday vs last year)?

The researchers discuss these and other factors which make learning easier or harder to transfer. Each one can vary along a continuum; transferring learning in a different laboratory would be harder than in the same laboratory, for example, but easier than outdoors. The factors also combine; a combination of a different topic/subject, location and stimulus, as well as a time delay, would make transfer very challenging indeed!

To some extent we can manage these factors for our students, but, again, it is worth considering *easier isn't necessarily better*. If we practise harder types of transfer (what researchers call *far transfer*), it will make it easier for students in the future. Ways to help students to transfer their learning during the initial practice stages include:

- giving hints and pointing out the similarities to previous tasks – for example, when showing students how to do a complicated mental maths problem, break it down into smaller sums previously that students have learnt how to solve;
- allowing them to try several tasks which have things in common, prompting reflection each time.

Build up the difficulty gradually, moving step by step from a similar task/application to a more distant one and providing scaffolding. For example, in business studies, a teacher might demonstrate the construction of a break-even graph from start to finish to the class so they can see the steps needed. This would then be followed up by guided practice where students individually construct a break-even graph in tandem with the teacher demonstrating each step one at a time. Students would then practise collaboratively with reduced teacher input and, finally, reach the stage where they can create a break-even graph independently.

Another way to tackle the difficulty of transfer is to include more variation in students practice, and this is discussed next.

## VARIATION AND COMPLEXITY

A further desirable difficulty is the extent to which practice tasks are *varied*. When practice is varied, learners become more accustomed to recognising how their learning can be applied and used in different ways. Again, this is not something accounted for in the multi-store model of memory, but the new theory of disuse helps us to understand that greater variation makes retrieval harder and storage more secure. The benefits to learning link mainly to overcoming some of the difficulties with transfer discussed above.

Some of the ways teachers can vary a task include:

- changing the academic context – for example, locating a principle within a scenario question, or engaging in project work or cross-curricular learning. For example, applying skills learnt in computing science lessons to another subject when creating digital media;
- using a different skill, such as switching from factual recall to application – for example, in history – instead of trying to recall verbally the facts of the events that occurred in the Hiroshima bombing, students could be asked to create a story board and discuss the role of this event in world peace movements;
- practising in a different physical location, such as learning outdoors, or setting a task as homework. For example, asking students to create a model of a mosque or church at home for their religious education lesson, labelling it to show the different aspects rather than simply drawing it in their exercise book or labelling a diagram;
- changing the social context, such as moving from individual work to group work. For example, students of politics could be asked to write notes on the dangers of fascism, and then discuss this in a group;
- being in a different mood or physical state. For example, in psychology, students might play a humorous revision game towards the end of the week, which would contrast with the more serious work done during practicals.

Delays lead to variation, so, while this is not the only benefit of the spacing effect, returning to an area of the curriculum a few months later will inevitably vary a number of things, such as the mood a learner is in, their level of knowledge and what they have been thinking about lately. Their social situation and the way the classroom looks might also be different.

Variation of practice is especially valuable with the most fundamental aspects of skills and knowledge, as these will crop up time and again. For example, most students will have a need for arithmetic skills, will need to operate a personal computer and will need to write. If such skills are practised in varied ways, they will be easier to apply flexibly when the need arises.

Granted, the future is inherently unpredictable. It can be hard to know *exactly* how our students might need to use a particular skill or fact they learn at school. If anything, though, this means varied practice is probably a good idea for *all* subjects and topics. It won't do any harm to learning, and can make it a lot more resilient if the need arises.

While useful for learning and transfer, variation will tend to negatively impact short-term performance. Just think how much worse you drive if you are in an unfamiliar car, or how much harder it is to play sport or cook with unfamiliar equipment! Again, it's important to make students aware of this. They need to understand that making more errors is not a bad thing – it's part of the process of developing a more resilient skill.

Related to the idea of variation is *complexity*. How complex are the practice tasks we give, in terms of the number of elements or 'moving parts'? A set of short-answer questions is less complex than a scenario question, which may in turn be less complex than an extended project. Of course, it's fine to use practice which is simplified in some way, especially in the early stages. But, at some point, it can help with transfer if tasks become more complex and authentic. If they don't, then they won't fully prepare learners for using their new knowledge and skills in the real world (beyond the exam).

For example:

- children in the early years practise with phonics and simplified texts, but the goal is for them to move on to independent reading;
- students who are new to a sport like basketball will practise movements, throws and footwork in an isolated way, but only so they can eventually put these skills together in the more complex context of a match.

## MANAGING DIFFICULTY

As difficulty increases, there has to be some consideration of student emotions, and ideally a bit of ownership on the part the learner – they need to understand and want these challenges. It is often best to make changes one step at a time; sometimes, new learning strategies may be unfamiliar to students. They should be encouraged to persevere, accepting short-term pain for long-term gain.

In the classroom, we often have to make a choice between a harder or a more straightforward practice task. At times, especially when learners are struggling for confidence or are new to the subject/topic, it might make sense to work on simpler tasks and build up to more challenging things (for more on this issue, see Chapter 6, where we discuss the issue of managing learner needs and modifying the difficulty level of various strategies).

Hopefully, if well managed, desirable difficulties will reduce anxiety over time and boost confidence as learners themselves realise they are improving and developing sound knowledge. Agarwal et al. (2014) found evidence that application of desirable difficulties such as retrieval practice reduces anxiety in school pupils, as the more they practise the better they become at retrieval and addressing any misconceptions. As noted by Dweck (2006), encouraging and praising students may lead to a fixation on performance (rather than learning). We should actively push students to take on challenges, and help them to understand that struggling at times is a normal part of learning. This education in 'how to learn' can support your use of desirable difficulties.

### REFLECTION POINT

Are there times when your learners seem a bit relaxed and the difficulty could be increased? And are there times when they are overwhelmed and anxious? Could a better understanding of how to learn help them to manage their anxiety?

## DIFFERENT STORES OF LTM

There is one further essential aspect of LTM that should be considered before concluding this chapter, and that relates to storage of different *types* of information (e.g., verbal, visual) that we remember. There are different ways to look at these:

- successors to the multi-store model tend to presume LTM has various stores – one for visual information, one for meaningful information and one for life events, among others;
- the idea of schemas suggests memories are interconnected. As conceived by Piaget and others, a schema includes not just factual information, but sensory and movement information (e.g., Piaget, 1950). It is assumed these are connected together into a kind of network.

Both of these ideas probably have at least an element of truth. An item can be stored differently depending on whether it is visual or verbal, and learners can retain something better if they encounter both verbal and visual information. This is called *dual coding* (Clark & Paivio, 1991). A YouTube video showing a historical moment is more memorable than trying to simply describe it or showing a static picture, a worksheet or whiteboard, and this is partly because it uses more than one sensory modality. Another example can be seen in Figure 3.3.

By extension, it is going to extend and enrich any form of learning if more sensory information is present in examples. The more examples and different types of sensory information learnt, the better chance the learner has of retaining one of them and thereby retrieving the knowledge that they need successfully. Exclusively using very simple and abstract forms won't be helpful.

At the same time, memories are interconnected. A simple example of this is that if you are shown an image of a piece of fruit, the word for that foodstuff will automatically spring to mind. So even if there are *separate stores* for visual and verbal information, they must be deeply interconnected. Richer knowledge in LTM will also influence processing in WM (see Chapter 2).

On a practical level, this means that we should be aiming to provide rich learning experiences, and that keeping things in very simple and abstract forms won't be helpful. Likewise, while verbal explanations are important; using other formats as part of the learning process is helpful too, such as stories.

Finally, the interconnected nature of memory brings us on to a discussion of the role of meaning. What exactly *is* meaning, and how does our learning become meaningful? What role does meaning play in the way things are retained in LTM – or forgotten? That will be the focus of the next chapter.

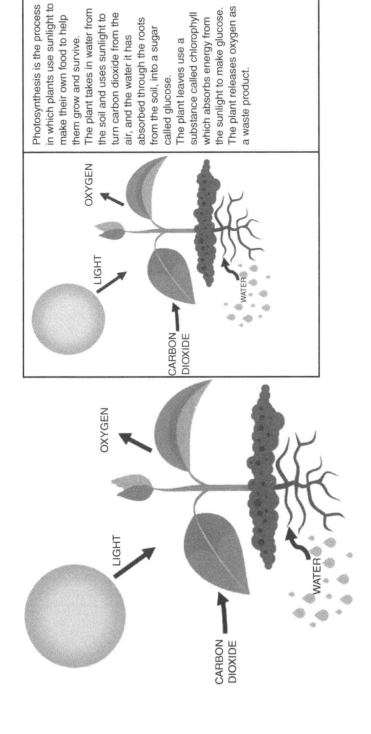

Photosynthesis is the process in which plants use sunlight to make their own food to help them grow and survive.

The plant takes in water from the soil and uses sunlight to turn carbon dioxide from the air, and the water it has absorbed through the roots from the soil, into a sugar called glucose.

The plant leaves use a substance called chlorophyll which absorbs energy from the sunlight to make glucose. The plant releases oxygen as a waste product.

OXYGEN

LIGHT

CARBON DIOXIDE

WATER

OXYGEN

LIGHT

CARBON DIOXIDE

WATER

**Figure 3.3** An example of dual coding

*Note*: adapted from Green Plant Sprout image by Vectorportal.com

# CONCLUSION

We have looked at some of the key features of long-term memory, focusing on two important theories – the multi-store model and the new theory of disuse. The multi-store model presents a helpful way of showing how LTM connects with working memory, and places an emphasis on how information is taken in and may be lost through forgetting.

However, as we have seen, this model is over simplistic. It assumes that repetition is the main way of getting information into LTM, and treats the two stores as largely separate in their functioning. The multi-store model also doesn't fully account for the spacing effect or active learning – both important factors in getting new learning to stick.

The new theory of disuse helpfully separates out the storage and retrieval strength of a memory, helping us to understand why things may be remembered today or tomorrow in class, but yet rapidly forgotten. That is to say, it emphasises learning rather than performance. To achieve learning, the model supports the use of desirable difficulties such as spacing and retrieval practice. These harm performance and lead to errors, but boost learning over the long term.

Finally, we saw how a key target for educators is that information transfers to other contexts, but that this is far from straightforward. Several strategies for boosting transfer are discussed, including varying the conditions of practice.

## KEY POINTS

- As with working memory, there are disagreements about LTM, including both how it is structured and how new information is encoded, stored and later retrieved or forgotten.
- Repetition is important, but it is not the whole story. Things can be repeated multiple times and still forgotten.
- Retention can be divided into two key components: storage and retrieval. Both are important, and educational strategies that focus on just one (retrieval, for example) are limited. To put it another way, learners need to be able to both retain things over the long term, and retrieve and use them when needed.
- Spacing out practice and making practice active (e.g., via active retrieval and application) helps to make sure information is secure in LTM rather than being rapidly

forgotten. These strategies can be applied to multiple areas of the curriculum (and beyond).

- Simplifying tasks for learners is not always the best way forward. Simpler tasks which are more similar to previous practice and more repetitive will be good for *performance*, but more complex tasks that are more similar to real life and more varied will be good for learning.
- Practice should (as far as possible) resemble the situation and conditions under which knowledge and skills will later be used.

# 4
# MEMORY AND CONCEPTUAL UNDERSTANDING

## INTRODUCTION

As we have seen in earlier chapters, a 20th-century view of long-term memory portrayed the mind as an information processer. Those who subscribed to this idea paid little attention to the meaning of what was being stored. More recent research has modified this basic model, and has clearly shown that the human mind is sensitive to meaning, demonstrating that information is remembered more easily if it is meaningful. In this chapter, we will explain how this affects lesson planning and teaching, and will explore related classroom concepts, including strategies that can be used for boosting meaningful understanding.

It's good to know that certain techniques can help to make information stick, but we cannot ignore the importance of what that information looks like and what it *means* to specific learners is a key part of the equation. Meaning helps things to be retained. A series of random words is clearly much harder to remember than something richly meaningful, like a story. Consider how easily you would remember an interesting anecdote from a friend, and, in comparison, how hard it would be to remember a page from a dull technical manual that you know nothing about.

Or, consider the following task:

### ACTIVITY

Try the following thought experiment. You have to read three sets of instructions for making a cup of tea (see below). The first is written in English, the second has words and phrases in English, but they have been scrambled, and appear in a random order and the third text has words in a language that is unfamiliar to you (we have used Turkish in the example, but if you speak Turkish, perhaps you can try to imagine what this would be like in an unfamiliar language!). Each time you are given two minutes to study the text, and are then tested on it. The amount of information is the same in all three instructions for making tea, as is the study time of two minutes.

| How to make a cup of tea (instructions) | How to make a cup of tea (jumbled up) | Bir fincan çay nasıl yapılır (in Turkish) |
| --- | --- | --- |
| 1. Fill up the kettle with water. | 1. Remove and dispose of the teabag. | 1. Su ısıtıcısını suyla doldurun. |
| 2. Boil the kettle. | 2. Boil the kettle. | 2. Su ısıtıcısını kaynatın. |
| 3. Place a teabag in your favourite mug. | 3. Pour boiling water into your favourite mug. | 3. Favori kupanıza bir poşet çay koyun. |
| 4. Pour boiling water into your favourite mug. | 4. Add sugar. | 4. En sevdiğiniz bardağa kaynar su dökün. |
| 5. Brew the tea for a few moments. | 5. Fill up the kettle with water. | 5. Çayı birkaç dakika demleyin. |
| 6. Remove and dispose of the teabag. | 6. Add milk. | 6. Çay poşetini çıkarın ve atın. |
| 7. Add milk. | 7. Brew the tea for a few moments. | 7. Süt ekleyin. |
| 8. Add sugar. | 8. Place a teabag in your favourite mug. | 8. Şeker ekleyin. |

Hopefully, the activity helps to show how *meaning* really matters. If tested on the sets of instructions, how accurately do you think you could write them from memory? We think that most people would find it much easier to remember the text in English written in order, because we understand it. We might remember some aspects of the second text, but probably only by making our own associations with the words or phrases, recognising that many of them are on a similar topic (making tea) and using that as the basis of a mnemonic (see Chapter 7), or otherwise coming up with ways to remember them. The third text would be very hard to remember indeed, as even the words themselves have little meaning for the reader (again, unless you are proficient in Turkish).

However, the amount of information is the same in all three situations, as is the study time. This demonstrates that input is not enough, and neither is repetition – there has to be understanding.

If we refer back to the multi-store model (see Chapter 3), you'll remember the idea that simply repeating things in working memory leads to them being encoded to long-term memory (LTM). These examples show that this theory falls down quite quickly if learners don't understand the information that they are attempting to memorise. If information doesn't make sense, you would struggle to recall it later, no matter how many times you repeat it to yourself.

The *new theory of disuse* (see Chapter 3) is much more helpful for classroom practice, as it emphasises the need to focus on lasting learning and be wary of techniques that boost temporary performance. The theory of disuse supports strategies such as spacing out and varying a learner's practice, as well as focusing on active retrieval as a means of consolidation simultaneously. However, this theory also has limitations; it doesn't tell us much about how memories link together, and there is a risk of looking at each memory as a separate item rather than as dependent on other ideas like a network.

Encoding and storing information in the LTM depends on meaning and involves developing your understanding and linking new ideas to what you already know. What's more, the more meaningful something is, the better you remember it. We will explore these ideas in this chapter, and consider what they imply for classroom practice.

# WHAT EXACTLY IS 'MEANING'?

The term 'meaning' may seem like a subjective concept. What is meaningful to one person is not necessarily meaningful to others. The task above for making tea in different languages demonstrates this. However, the task also shows that we can recognise the role of meaning when we see it. And, overall, researchers do in fact have a pretty good idea of how meaning works and what specifically makes something meaningful.

## SOME KEY FEATURES OF MEANING

Let's consider a few features that have emerged from the points so far.

### Meaning can occur at different levels of depth
In the activity above you understood the words and phrases of tea-making when these were written in order and in a language you recognise and understand. However, it would be more meaningful still if tea was especially important to you,

and it would be less meaningful if you have only a superficial understanding of what tea is (to a very young child, for example). On a very shallow level, you understood the words from the text in a scrambled order, even if not the full message.

### Meaning relates to what is already in LTM

This is why it's harder to retain information from a 'dry' technical manual than an anecdote. Someone who has never made a cup of tea before or used the utensils would struggle to take in the main ideas from the task. It would be similar if you read an article about an unfamiliar sport. As a further example (again dependent on your personal experience), try reading the text in the following activity, which explains the first stage of the Lakshmi Puja Vidhi, a special prayer during Diwali. Relevant background knowledge will affect making sense of these and other texts.

## ACTIVITY

Consider the following text. What does it tell you about prior knowledge and meaning?

Puja should begin with the meditation of Bhagawati Lakshmi. Dhyana should be done in front of already installed Shri Lakshmi statue in front of you. Following Mantra should be chanted while meditating on Bhagawati Shri Lakshmi.

### Meaning can be personal

What we as authors find meaningful may not be meaningful to you as a reader, and vice versa. This is because everyone has different knowledge and experiences which help them to make sense of new information, and their own set of emotional responses. This is, of course, true of students as well.

### Meaning can be an active and constructive process

English psychologist Bartlett (1932) referred to this as 'effort after meaning'. We make sense of things, imposing a meaning even when there isn't one there. People might put together words and phrases from the jumbled instructions in the first activity to make a story, for example. In other words, people try to make sense of incoming information.

### Meaning is based on interests

Everyone has a sense of curiosity and likes to solve a puzzle, but it makes a difference if you have a good reason to want to know the answer to that puzzle. As teachers, we try to ignite the curiosity of our learners, inviting them to consider information because they want to know the answer to the questions or find out what happened next. For example, when teaching students about Martin Luther King in history, student curiosity helps them to make sense of the events and prompts them to find out more about what happened to Dr King, and to retain it.

A connected structure of information is easier to remember than separate pieces of information. A sentence is easier to remember than separate words in a list, and a longer text is easier to remember than a bunch of random sentences. We may be more likely to remember information or examples if they are told to us in story form, or connected to an anecdote. For example, we are more likely to remember the first stage of the Lakshmi Puja Vidhi (see the second activity) if a friend explains their own experience of it.

Bruner (1990) referred to the human mind as 'a meaning-maker', suggesting that as a species we are fundamentally set up to make sense of our surroundings, not to process information like a computer. Overall, then, meaning is complex, but also fundamental to how we think and act. There really isn't an aspect of everyday human life where it doesn't matter.

## HOW THE MIND ORGANISES INFORMATION

*Constructivism* is a theory from education and psychology which states that information isn't processed and taken in as if the mind were a blank slate. Instead, learners *build up* (construct) new learning on the basis of what they already know. It is a cumulative, active process.

It is a constructivist perspective to suggest that existing knowledge affects what we find meaningful. This means that learners can't take things into memory successfully without understanding them, and the way that they understand new facts and ideas is by linking them to existing knowledge (Piaget, 1950; Wittrock, 1974). New information also impacts on these mental structures and causes the learner to rethink and reorganise what they know.

An essential idea from the theory of constructivism is the concept of the 'schema'. As explained in Chapter 1, a schema is a set of knowledge and ideas that is bundled together into a single concept. Unlike a computer, the way the human mind stores what it knows can't be broken down into isolated bits of data. Instead, we relate old information to new, and the knowledge that we have gradually builds up.

Each concept in the learner's mind – for example, of a business, a rainforest, or a desert biome – can get gradually more complex as they encounter more examples. Learners link in relevant emotions and actions as their schemas develop over time. They also learn to distinguish contrasting examples, to better categorise new examples, allowing their schemas to be subdivided. Each schema a learner has is different; it differs from knowledge in that knowledge is universal and a schema is personal.

The schema concept has certain implications for the classroom.

1. When we take in new information, it can be *assimilated*, meaning that it is mentally categorised and linked to an existing schema. For example, in chemistry, students learn to categorise new substances as acids or bases, depending on their chemical properties.
2. A schema can provide a learner with prototypical information about a concept. For example, if young learners are asked to 'draw a bird', they typically draw a small flying bird, not an ostrich or a penguin.
3. As learners become more sophisticated and knowledgeable, their schemas get correspondingly more complex, with many examples and details that they can draw upon.
4. When a learner takes in information that doesn't quite fit an existing schema, it prompts them to rethink and reorganise their understanding. Perhaps a child sees a tram running along the street. This causes dissonance because, according to their *train* schema, trains have their own special lines and they don't run on streets like a car. The child may then be told that this vehicle is called a tram. Gradually they start to form a new schema for *trams*, but one that is closely linked to their existing *trains* schema.

Taking account of these principles, we can plan the curriculum as a 'spiral', helping learners to develop ever more sophisticated schemas as they go up through the school years. This is commonly framed in terms of 'learning journeys' which aim to show students how topics will build on prior learning. For example, in secondary school, we may start academic Year 1 by teaching students how to program using Python in their computing science lessons. We could then develop this further as students progress, adding more knowledge to their existing knowledge and showing them how to write more complicated programs before moving on to the fundamentals of algorithms. Further on still, students could be asked to complete a programming project of their own (see Table 4.1).

**Table 4.1**    An example of building student schemas through revisiting topics

|  |  | Year 9 | Year 10 | Year 11 |
|---|---|---|---|---|
| **Half term 1** | Topics | Programming | Fundamentals of algorithms | Programming project Data representation |
|  | Knowledge | Coding Python | Step-by-step plans for solving problems | Analysing the data Tackling the exam AQA project |
| **Half term 2** | Topics | Fundamentals of computer networks | Fundamentals of data representation | Fundamentals of algorithms |
|  | Knowledge | Packets and data: the sending of data | Compression and encoding data Worked out exam questions | Step-by-step plans for solving problems Applying to the AQA project |
| **Half term 3** | Topics | Fundamentals of data representation | Programming Computer networks: the hardware | Cyber security: Managing Incidents. |
|  | Knowledge | Storing images Increasing colour depth Storing and affecting sound quality | Router, IP address Switches packet and hardware | Measures to protect against CS incidents Understand how to manage CS incidents |
| **Half term 4** | Topics | Computer systems Programming | Programming concept | Computer networks Computer systems |
|  | Knowledge | Components and application OS | Solving problems using coding programming languages | Benefits and limitations of each network on given computer systems |
| **Half term 5** | Topics | Fundamentals of cyber security | Programming project, software development | Exam revision |
|  | Knowledge | Understanding issues that surround CS Securing data and devices | Computational thinking | Exam revision |
| **Half term 6** | Topics | Ethical, legal and environmental | Computer systems | Exam |
|  | Knowledge | The ethical side of computing | System software and utilities Worked exam questions | Exam |

Overall, it is important to understand that students will have different schemas with different levels of complexity and elaboration. This means that they begin a task at different starting points. It is worth exploring the starting point of students in the lesson through effective questioning before teaching an idea. These differences also mean that:

- students will categorise and organise new information differently depending on their prior exposure to the ideas being discussed;
- some will be able to come up with ideas that others won't;
- some will notice key distinctions that others won't;
- they will come up with different prototypical examples, when prompted.

Research has shown that cultural differences and differences in social class are important factors in these issues. It is worth bearing in mind how this different background knowledge may put some learners at a disadvantage when accessing teaching, reading, or examples. Using multiple examples may go some way towards addressing this.

## REFLECTION POINT

Can you recall a time from your own studies when you interpreted something differently from your classmates? Could schemas help to explain this?

Extending the above points, when learners go through the process of becoming an expert on a topic they develop highly complex, subdivided and interconnected schemas on that topic. This helps them to recognise subtleties that a beginner would miss.

When a learner reads or hears about something, a relevant schema (or schemas) may or not be active. If a schema is active, then the new information is more easily recognised and categorised. If it is not active, then they may miss the point, and fail to make relevant connections. This is one of the reasons that teachers often begin a lesson with a starter task or quiz that reminds students about relevant prior learning. They are activating relevant schemas and checking for misconceptions before they go any further with the learning.

Schemas also become activated by context. In a classic research study, just using an image made learners better able to take in verbal information; an informative headline could play a similar role (Bransford & Johnson, 1972).

## ACTIVITY

Write a short list of starter tasks that would help to activate schemas in your teaching, in order to better prepare learners for subsequent new knowledge.

## COSTS OF SCHEMAS

While schemas are essential for learners to organise information, the way they function does come with certain costs to the individual. A research study in the 1980s (Brewer & Treyens, 1981) showed both the memory benefits and the costs of schemas clearly. In the study, participants were asked to wait in an office, which had been prepared in advance with some schema-relevant objects (such as a desk chair or a telephone) as well as some more unusual objects that are not typically found in an office (such as a skull or a picnic basket).

After waiting for a couple of minutes, learners were led into another room, and asked to write down everything that they had seen in the office. The researchers found that people tended to remember schema-relevant objects (such as the telephone) and forget schema-irrelevant objects (such as the picnic basket). Participants hadn't known in advance that they would be tested on the objects, so hadn't made an effort to memorise them.

This study shows that while things that fit our schemas enter memory more easily, things that do not are likely to be forgotten. This effect is similar to the earlier points about students sometimes not understanding (and therefore not remembering) certain types of information we have taught them from one lesson to another.

There is also a broad research literature that suggests that what we recall is often biased by assumptions of various kinds (e.g., Loftus, 1996). A stereotype is a type of schema, for example, and stereotypes can affect what people perceive and remember (or *believe* they remember). It's much easier for individuals to think about and remember information that fits their schema – these associations come more easily. So, when educators try to tackle prejudice as part of citizenship education or address potential misconceptions in other subject areas, it is best if they have a clear idea of how schemas work.

# STRATEGIES FOR BOOSTING MEANINGFUL UNDERSTANDING

We have seen so far that schemas are fundamental structures and networks of existing information around which memories are meaningfully organised within a learner's mind.

As shown in the case of assumptions and stereotypes, categorising of knowledge and learners' prior knowledge influencing their thinking is not something that educators have a choice about. It will happen whether we like it or not. Our learners will link things into their own existing schemas, and this will sometimes contribute to errors and misconceptions, especially if they have different experiences to their teachers.

For example, in business studies students have some concepts of customer service so we can use this existing knowledge of what is good and bad customer service in class. Students who have never experienced poor customer service may need more prompting as to why this is an issue to the success of the business.

Clearly, it is desirable for learners have more complete schemas, and ones that help them to think in sophisticated, creative and, above all, *accurate* ways. So, what should educators do to assist with this? The following sections focus on two key issues.

## MISCONCEPTIONS AND CONTRASTS

First, teachers can try to improve the accuracy of what their learners know and believe. This can have its roots in careful planning – for example, using a scheme of learning. Teachers are also best to engage in careful prior questioning or quizzing, which is not only useful as retrieval practice strategy, but also as a formative assessment technique to check student starting points and highlight common errors.

After a classroom task, it is important not to assume what you have taught the class (as you understand it) is the message that students have actually received. Checking understanding and questioning at key points in the lesson is critical to ensure students are following and understanding the material as intended.

Most new teachers soon become aware of common misconceptions in their subject(s). We can draw attention to areas of confusion, which teachers often do by highlighting common misconceptions and by giving feedback that highlights meaningful mistakes.

Misconceptions can bounce back, because learners retain both their initial ideas and their new learning in memory. Teachers should therefore return to these misconceptions and probe for them in the context of problems or scenarios.

We can also work to emphasise *contrasts*. When learners are asked to contrast two confusable things – two things that look superficially similar but have important differences – it makes it easier to notice and remember those differences. For example, the difference between 'weather' and 'climate' in geography is a common area of confusion, and new learners may use the terms interchangeably. Later, geography students might learn about the different types of clouds. In these examples, contrasting the differences directly will help learners to remember them because this work helps to ensure that information is meaningfully categorised.

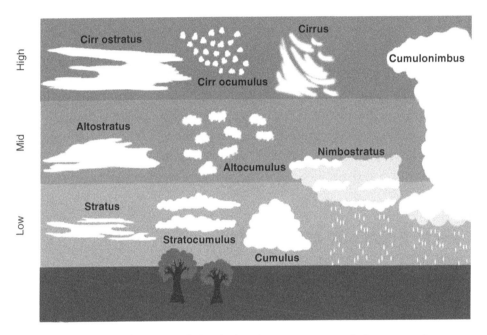

**Figure 4.1**    Example of the types of clouds that learners may study in geography

## INTERLEAVING

Another promising technique that appears to help with the development of new concept knowledge is *interleaving*. This means varying the order of examples or tasks, so that learners see contrasting types of items together. It differs from standard educational practice; more often, students are given sets of examples or practice problems that all illustrate the *same* concept or skill.

Interleaving benefits from both drawing student attention to issues and from contrast (see previous section). Indeed, interleaving the order of items is a way of building these two processes into the task itself. By showing easily confused items or examples side by side, we draw learners' attention to the differences in a way that wouldn't happen if they appeared in different study sessions. We also highlight contrasts by making them more salient.

The kind of items that might be interleaved in the classroom include verbal examples, short problems or tasks and visual images. When the order of these items is interleaved, it means that each one is preceded and followed by examples of a *different* concept. An interleaved worksheet might include some questions on the current topic of fractions and some extra questions on equations and multiplication from a previous lesson.

Showing examples of different concepts all together in one task or worksheet might sound confusing. After all, teachers often want to present areas of the curriculum one at a time, giving learners time for practice of a single new idea before moving on to the next thing. However, interleaving actually helps learners to refine their essential schema-based knowledge. It helps them to get their head around the limits of a concept. Consider this: a learner needs to know what something *is not*, as well as what it *is*.

To give a concrete example, consider a learner in geography looking at types of rocks – for example, igneous rocks. To learn about this kind of rock, it would be useful for the student to see various examples of what igneous rock can look like, but also to see rocks that are *not* igneous, in order to highlight the differences. The ideal order to learn about types of rock would be to interleave multiple easily confused types in a single episode of learning.

In English, a learner may be looking at similes, metaphors and analogies. To understand the differences between these three figures of speech, it is often best to show them together, so that the contrast between them is more obvious.

### Interleaving vs blocking

As discussed above, an interleaved presentation involves alternating the order between items from different categories, usually brief examples or images. For example, an interleaved order to show pictures of the five main types of frog found in the UK (common frog, northern pool frog, marsh frog, edible frog, bull frog) might go:

common/northern/marsh/edible/bull/common/northern/marsh/edible/bull
… and so on.

Evidence has shown that an interleaved order leads to learners being more accurately able to categorise new, previously unseen examples of an animal species

(Birnbaum et al., 2013). Researchers describe a set of *similar* examples/items – ones from the same category – as a *blocked* presentation, for example:

common/common/common; northern/northern/northern; marsh/marsh/marsh, etc. ...

In such a set, it is not the item that is repeated, but the *category*. Learners are being given another example of the same kind of thing – a different image of the same species of frog, for example. This is less helpful for learning to correctly categorise new examples.

**Table 4.2**    Interleaved vs blocked approaches across the curriculum

| Blocked | Interleaved |
|---|---|
| A lesson on art by a single artist | Studying paintings by two or more artists within the same lesson, e.g., Salvador Dali and Henri Matisse |
| Studying the rainforest in one country | Studying the rainforest in several parts of the world, to understand the differences |
| Looking at examples of one group of chemicals, e.g., alcohols | Looking at examples of two or more groups of chemicals, e.g., alcohols vs alkenes |
| Looking at how Victorian Britain enforced law and order | Looking at examples of approaches to law and order from several countries or from several eras |
| Looking at many examples of graphics processors in a computer | Comparing images of graphics processors with other superficially similar components |
| Studying acids in one lesson and bases in another lesson | Comparing the properties of acidic, alkaline and neutral chemicals |

Hopefully, the examples in Table 4.2 further illustrate the most important purpose of interleaving – that an interleaved order of items draws attention to and highlights contrasts between different categories. As the breadth of the examples show, this can potentially apply right across the curriculum.

There are occasions where it would make more sense to give a set of examples in a blocked order. The reason for this comes back to the idea of drawing learner attention to contrasts. Doing so only makes sense if the contrasts are subtle, and easily missed. No learner is going to mix up a bird with a fish, or a poem with a crime novel. These categories are already so obviously different that it doesn't make sense for a teacher to highlight the differences. If a set of examples have things *in common* which are easily missed, the reverse logic starts to hold. In this case, it would be best to block such a set of items, to help draw attention to their similarities.

This might be a less common situation, but it is nevertheless important, and shows why it is important for teachers to understand interleaving and its link to schemas, rather than just to apply it to every situation.

A good practical example might be the concept of 'revolution' in history and politics. What is a revolution, and what is not? Historical revolutions may look superficially quite different to the learner, but they have subtle and important aspects in common. In this case, blocking the examples could be a useful approach. Carvalho and Goldstone (2014) explain that the level of similarity among a set of items is what should help us as teachers to determine whether we should interleave or not.

A way to cut through the possible confusion about when to block and when to interleave examples is to use your professional knowledge to think about where confusion generally arises in your subject/classroom at the planning stages of writing the curriculum teaching plan. What do learners struggle to understand in your subject? Where do they get mixed up? What subtle similarities/commonalities do they miss? Interleaving is a good strategy for tackling such confusion.

## REFLECTION POINT

What are the major areas of confusion that arise in your teaching subject? If a set of items are *subtly* different, it would be best to interleave them, so that learners notice the differences. If the set of items are *obviously* different, learners might actually find it hard to notice the similarities, rather than the differences! To see what such items have in common, it would be best to study them in a block, rather than to interleave.

Overall, if learners tend to miss subtle differences in a topic, use interleaving. If they tend to fail to spot underlying *similarities*, use blocking.

Interleaving is an idea that can be applied to classrooms at every age and stage. The main difference for more advanced learners is that the differences that they notice become more subtle, for exactly the reasons discussed earlier in this chapter – they know more and therefore have more complex and sophisticated schemas.

Hopefully, these points show that while the benefits of interleaving are certainly powerful, they do require some professional judgement and awareness of the key issues, both in terms of the material and the learners themselves. These are not techniques that we can always apply to every situation, but rather a part of an educator's professional toolbox.

And remember – we have to use some order or other! The scheduling of items is not an issue we can sidestep. Often, though, the default order for items will be blocked, because of the tendency to categorise like with like. Using more interleaving can be a good way to get learners to appreciate differences that they would otherwise miss.

### The case of practice problems and techniques

Most of what has been said so far about interleaving and blocking applies to things like science or social science concepts, or other subjects where brief examples can be given (see Table 4.2).

However, interleaving can also be applied to practice problems of the type that might feature in the maths or physics classroom and, indeed, there is a strong research basis to suggest that it is useful in these contexts too.

- First, the interleaved examples may provide useful discriminative contrast between different types of problem, as is the case with interleaved examples and images. For example, they benefit from interleaving tasks which involve multiplying fractions with tasks that involve dividing fractions.
- Second, as explained by Doug Rohrer and colleagues (Rohrer et al., 2015), interleaved problems provide the learner with practice in selecting the right strategy or technique. And this is often what they are expected to do in tests and exams. As such, interleaved practice of maths problems is much more effective as a means of learning the subject than simply repeating the same technique again and again.

Unfortunately, repetition of the same technique appears to be the standard practice in classrooms and in textbooks, meaning that students will be getting fewer opportunity to contrast different problem types. In a later study, Rohrer and colleagues (Rohrer et al., 2020) reviewed the examples in a number of mainstream maths textbooks and found that interleaved examples are scarce – the norm is to block by type.

Such textbooks are placing an emphasis on repetition and overlearning. Both techniques are widespread and often recommended. However, as explained in the previous chapter, repetition is not a reliable way to encode knowledge to LTM. And overlearning is inefficient over the long term.

### The case of independent study

It might occur to you that if interleaving works in the classroom, it should be applied to student's independent study. Some teachers and schools do now advocate for it as an evidence-based strategy and encourage their students to include interleaving as part of their toolkit of study techniques. We see this commonly as revision topic timetables which are interleaved and attempts to demonstrate the effectiveness of this to students.

However, there are difficulties with this. One issue is that to make the best use of discriminative contrast requires a certain level of expertise. Research studies that show the strongest interleaving effects tend to contrast carefully chosen examples – ones selected by researchers to be subtly different. Can learners identify such subtle contrasts for themselves and arrange their study notes in order to highlight these? It seems that (almost by definition), novices are unaware of these subtle differences. If so, they will struggle to organise their study materials accordingly (and may choose to contrast the wrong things).

In subjects where revision features a lot of short practice problems, perhaps including multiple choice, it may be easier for learners to interleave independently. They can attempt to shuffle their topics and proceed on the basis of 'like follows unlike' rather than 'like follows like'. But, again, there are difficulties. How different do two practice problems need to be in order to gain the benefit of contrast? This is a highly technical question and there is some doubt as to whether novice learners can organise a set of practice problems in the optimal order for themselves. In both cases, it seems to us, it would be far better for teachers to bring their experience to bear on the problem and to produce sets of study materials that make the best use of interleaving.

One possible exception is with flashcards. When students make flashcards for themselves (a technique which is ideal for self-testing and therefore for retrieval practice), it would be simple for them to shuffle the cards, thereby mixing together different topics.

However, the research on how best to interleave flashcards (or whether to do so at all!) is still ongoing, meaning that there is no clear research consensus at this point. One useful study by Hausman and Kornell (2014) failed to find a benefit of shuffling together unrelated topics (biology and modern language vocabulary). This is perhaps unsurprising, as there would be no useful contrasts between the different items. However, neither did it make matters worse.

Overall, as things stand, it would appear that the main uses of flashcards are unrelated to interleaving, and advice to students should instead focus on spacing out their practice, and on doing retrieval in the most effective way. Given the lack of supporting research evidence for shuffling flashcards of different subjects and topics, advice to interleave flashcards is probably an unnecessary distraction, and one that students will struggle to understand.

We will explore the implications of memory principles for independent study in more detail in Chapter 7.

## OVERLEARNING

As mentioned above, overlearning is a technique which is widespread in education and often recommended, but can be seen as inefficient over the long term. Technically, overlearning means learning beyond the point of mastery. But what is mastery, exactly?

Drawing on the concepts studied in the previous chapter, we can say that mastery (at least in a school/college context) means studying to the point of being able to retrieve something fluently and without excessive effort or cognitive load (see Chapter 2). It needn't imply permanent learning but does show successful *performance*. If a student can answer a question on a concept or execute a skill, and then do three or four relevant problems correctly, they could be said to have mastered the concept at that moment in time.

As noted, the common classroom practice in many subjects is to provide long lists of practice tasks that try to reinforce a particular learning outcome. Such an approach may seem to make sense; fundamentally, it reflects behaviourism – a theory of learning which promoted the idea that learning involves a lot of practice, with feedback, until something sticks. It is therefore associated with techniques that emphasise repetition (along with things like rote repetition and drilling). An analogy is that such practice techniques aim to hammer home an idea as firmly as possible.

It doesn't fit as well with certain key principles of memory that we have looked at so far and, as teachers, we need to consider this when planning lessons and tasks. Encoding to LTM is not based purely on repetition, while depth of meaningful understanding – as we have seen in this chapter – is a fundamental aspect of memory and retention. Repeating the same type of thing again and again is not the way to make it more meaningful.

Furthermore, overlearning conflicts with the idea of interleaving, as it tends to involve repetition of the same type of problem. It conflicts with the spacing effect (see Chapter 3). These issues suggest an important discrepancy between research into memory and certain traditional classroom approaches.

It's perhaps no surprise, then, to find that recent experimental studies have disputed the benefits of overlearning. In their classic study of retrieval practice, researchers Roediger and Karpicke (2006) found a short boost in test scores if participants read a text over *twice* rather than just *once* – but this benefit was only apparent on a test that occurred within five minutes. A week later, it was participants who had actively engaged with and retrieved the information who did better on a test.

Rohrer and Taylor (2006) directly compared the effect of pupils doing a short set of maths tasks versus a long one. In both cases, pupils had reached 90 per cent mastery after the first three tasks. One group proceeded to do another six problems of the same type – nine in total. They were all then tested after a delay; there was no difference between the groups. This is remarkable, considering that one group had spent around three times as long on practice!

These findings show that the benefits of overlearning, if any, are temporary. They support the idea that it would be much better for teachers to spread out practice over time (spacing), to interleave problems with others of contrasting types and to engage in deeper, more meaningful learning rather than repetition of things that have already been mastered.

These points are not always obvious, however. Many teachers believe that overlearning is a valuable strategy, and fail to appreciate how inefficient it is in terms of how study time is used. Likewise, many students will overestimate the impact of re-reading as a study strategy, even though any boost to performance tends to quickly disappear with time.

## REFLECTION POINT

Instead of overlearning, learners should stop when they have reached mastery and return to do further practice at a later date (i.e., they should engage in spaced practice). Has this been the case during your own education?

And what about the materials that you currently use when teaching? Is it common practice in your subject to have long lists of tasks that aim at overlearning the same point? If so, could some of these be modified to incorporate spacing and/or interleaving?

As explained above earlier, interleaving is one way to boost the development of learners' schemas, making it an important alternative to repetition and overlearning. But there are other approaches that can be considered, drawing on some of the points made earlier in the chapter. The following techniques all focus on deepening learners' meaningful understanding of the topics at hand:

- *self-explanation*: this is where a learner explains a concept to themselves. The process of doing so helps to strengthen links within and between schemas;
- *elaborative interrogation*: similar to the above, this is when the learner asks themselves questions about an issue, seeking to understand key issues and distinctions;
- *summarisation*: this is when the learner attempts to produce a simplified over-view that includes the main idea in a set of notes. A summary, written after a delay, is a feature of Cornell note-taking;
- *imagery*: this is when visual images are used to help make learning more con-crete, and to benefit from dual coding – the mind's ability to retain visual images alongside notes better than notes alone.

Self-explanation and elaborative interrogation are more effective than summarisation or imagery (Dunlosky et al., 2013), though the latter techniques could be used in combination with spacing, and a focus placed on depth of meaning. Reading more widely around their school subject(s) may also help to deepen students' knowledge, boosting not only their current competence but their readiness for future learning.

Overall, such approaches help to tackle the tendency to focus on shallow, repetition-focused strategies, and to start to build deep, flexible, usable knowledge.

### REFLECTION POINT

What study habits have you used (and recommended) in the past, and do they focus on meaning?

In terms of guiding learners, have you noticed some of your students incorrectly assuming that repetition and overlearning are useful study strategies? If so, could they instead be guided to space out their practice and use more active and meaning-focused techniques?

## CONCLUSION

In this chapter, we have seen that techniques for embedding things into memory are not the whole story. To make learning last, we also need to consider learners' mean-ingful understanding. In particular, teachers should be suspicious of approaches that focus on rote repetition.

Meaning is a hard concept to define, but, as we have seen, it has various recognisable features. In particular, meaning depends heavily on a learner's existing knowledge, structured as schemas.

We have also seen that a schema is dynamic and can change over time as a learner encounters more examples and fuller information. Learners use schemas as mental categories, helping them to make sense of new information. But schemas are also a source of misconceptions that may need to be tackled in your subject. To tackle misconceptions, it is valuable to focus learners' attention on differences, especially subtle ones, and to highlight contrasts. A technique that builds in contrast and boosts attention is known as interleaving – shuffling the order of examples so that *like* appears with *unlike*. However, learners won't always have the awareness to use this technique successfully in their independent study.

Finally, we saw that overlearning is a flawed technique, again based on repetition rather than meaningful understanding. It is preferable for teachers to build in delays (spacing) and also to use techniques such as self-explanation that focus on deepening learners' meaningful understanding.

## KEY POINTS

- Techniques like spacing and retrieval are important, but educators can't ignore the importance of meaningful understanding.
- Psychologists tend to view memories as being structured into schemas rather than as separate items.
- Previous knowledge can help learners to take in new information, especially if these schemas are 'activated'.
- Interleaving is a technique which involves contrasting examples of different but easily confused concepts.
- Interleaving can be applied to sets of practice problems. It is more effective than overlearning of sets of problems.
- Students' misconceptions can lead them astray, meaning that they need guidance on using interleaving in the classroom, and may not always select meaning-focused study techniques.
- Overlearning is not long-lasting in its effects, while techniques that focus on deepening learners' meaningful understanding are better supported by research evidence.

# 5

# APPLYING MEMORY TO EVERYDAY TEACHING PRACTICE

## INTRODUCTION

How do students and teachers use their memories on an everyday basis? This chapter expands on the ideas raised in previous chapters by exploring various teaching activities where good memory storage and memory strategies play a role.

As teachers, we spend a lot of time planning and thinking about how best to prepare lesson content and tasks to support our students at all levels and abilities. It's now time to take a step back to the lesson planning process and think about what you, the teacher, can do to enhance your everyday classroom practice to enable students to better retain their learning and recall information when it is needed.

We will consider what memory looks like in the classroom, from the perspective of planning and classroom pedagogy right through to consolidation activities. In each case, we will tease apart the memory processes that take place in the classroom, and link them back to the ideas we have discussed from the previous chapters – specifically the stores and processes of memory.

The subtleties of memory can make it a challenging concept to grasp, but it becomes much easier to understand when put into context. As a teacher, this means how memory processes and stores affect everyday learning tasks – the kind of things that we see and recognise happening every day in our classrooms. In closely linking and comparing your developing knowledge of memory to what is happening in everyday practice, you will more fully appreciate the key concepts that we have explored so far and be better able to recognise and apply them. In other words, the focus here is on the changes or tweaks that can be made to the teaching activities or strategies you already use to make them more effective for learning.

## ACTIVITY

Think about some of the areas in your learning context where students sometimes struggle. What is it that they find difficult? What do they find easy?

## ACTIVE LEARNING

Before we delve into the specific types of classroom activities and tasks and their links to memory, it is worth taking a moment to consider the meaning of a term that is widely used in education, and which was briefly touched on in Chapter 3: *active learning*. Most teachers will say that they want learning to be active, but what exactly does this mean ... and what are the benefits of incorporating active learning in our planning?

Being 'active' is sometimes assumed by teachers and students to involve learning via particular physical apparatus or materials. Perhaps we envisage a situation where learners are working together, moving around the room, drawing pictures or posters, or using physical materials, for example. Learning about the difference between plant and animal cells in biology via a textbook or a video would not tend to be classed as active learning. However, the same objectives could perhaps be achieved by other means. A teacher may feel that they should take a more hands-on approach, perhaps they would ask students to compare onion cells with cells from the inside of their cheek using iodine.

Practical experiments and tasks can certainly be memorable, in part because they are varied, and support transfer (see Chapter 3) and we are certainly not trying to discourage their use. However, the most important impact on memory comes when learners are *cognitively* active. What are learners thinking about when they engage with a task? And to what extent do they need to think for themselves, rather than having a teacher think for them? Two people can sit through the same lecture or video, with one being much more cognitively active than the other! It's not always the activity that counts, but the way that learners engage with it. This can include follow-up tasks, such as having learners engage in self-explanation of what they found (see Chapter 4) as homework.

Retrieval practice is a good example of active learning. It isn't typically based on movement, but rather on *doing* something with the information – recalling it, perhaps after a delay and perhaps in an unfamiliar context. For example, in modern languages, students may have learnt how to introduce themselves and their family, and be learning to talk about their hobbies and interests. In a few lessons time, students may be asked to listen to a recording of a native French speaker talking about themselves and asked to pick out key pieces of information. They may later be asked to translate a text written in English to demonstrate they can apply their new language speaking and reading skills to a range of situations. As students retrieve and organise the information in their mind, there is more of a demand on them to think deeply. This type of active learning helps students not only to retrieve their prior learning but also to apply it to other contexts.

Research by Saskia Giebl and colleagues (Giebl et al., 2021) shows how much this matters. They found that most learners will tend to google or otherwise look up information, even if they have already studied it. If they instead take a moment to think about the information, it is beneficial to their learning over the long term. This is true even if they don't recall it successfully! Even an attempt to recall the facts makes us more cognitively active, and more receptive to later learning.

## REFLECTION POINT

Consider how you learn the names of a class of students. You might be using the names correctly after the first lesson, but this can be described as performance rather than learning. It needs consolidation. So, what do you do next time around? Read the names on your class list/register or attempt to actively recall them from memory? The study by Giebl et al. (2021) suggests that the latter strategy would be more effective.

We know that long-term memory depends on organising material well, linking it to existing schemas (see Chapters 1 and 4) and encoding it in multiple different contexts (Smith et al., 1978). Active learning may also involve other factors that promote better understanding, such as applying knowledge to a practical task, varying the setting in which information is used or applied, or other forms of problem solving. In promoting deep thinking, such activities help learners to remember better, too. We will return to some of these issues in later chapters, but for now, it is worth considering that tasks which promote cognitive activity will tend to lead to more secure encoding in LTM. This translates into enhanced learning and better application of knowledge to new contexts.

## SCENARIO 5.1

Mrs A teaches business studies. When teaching the types of business ownership, she explains the differences between private and public limited companies using a ten-minute block of 'talk through' time, making it clear to the students that they only need to concentrate and listen for that time. The material learning is then consolidated with an active task. Mrs A believes that this helps to balance the importance of new factual information with opportunities to use and actively make sense of the information.

## CLASSROOM STRATEGIES

### LISTENING TO EXPLANATIONS

How does information enter memory in the first place? Perhaps the oldest form of teaching of all is to *tell* people things. The example from Scenario 5.1 shows how a verbal explanation can usefully precede a more active task. Verbally explaining things to learners is a strategy used in every kind of teaching from physical education to science to art, at every age group and in every culture around the world.

While 'telling' is only one of many possible strategies, it can't be denied that it is potentially a useful way of getting information across to a class, especially with large numbers of students. For many teachers, it seems the surest way to cover curriculum content in a clear manner within a limited time frame. As it targets a whole group of learners simultaneously, the technique has the potential to be both quick and efficient.

At the same time, it could reasonably be pointed out that although verbal explanations are efficient, that doesn't always make them effective from a learning perspective. Listening to a lecture or video, for example, is often quite a passive activity, and we've all been in the position where someone begins a boring family anecdote or tells us a set of directions, and a minute later we've completely lost the thread. When that happens, nothing useful will be going into LTM. We can sometimes see this in the classroom with students drifting off into their own thoughts.

Likewise, we've probably all been in situations where we have experienced a sense of information overload. When reading a book like this, you can pause to think, taking in information at your own pace. In a lecture or at an education conference, things move at *the speaker's* pace. Unless a talk is particularly well-designed, there is often very little time for consolidation, not to mention application or problem solving. As teachers, we shouldn't underestimate the importance of these active processes in allowing the information to be understood and linked to existing schemas.

Perhaps because of these issues, some figures in education discourage 'teacher talking time'. We are sure that at some point you will have heard colleagues explaining how this was frowned upon during their initial education/training, or even anecdotes about student teachers being failed outright for talking too much in class!

While we don't agree that arbitrary limits should be put on this strategy, there is a sensible idea behind it. It's fair to say that students have a limited attention span, and even those learners who are well motivated may at times fail to pay attention, instead engaging in natural mind-wandering as they become overwhelmed (see Chapter 2 for more about mind-wandering!).

From a memory point of view, these issues raise some important points and principles for the classroom:

- direct instruction and lecturing are a useful and efficient tool for sharing information with a whole class. However, they rely on students using their working memory to take in and process the new information and, in particular, linking the information to prior knowledge or schemas;
- distractions could affect these processes, and the effectiveness of the strategy may depend on how the information is structured, or what the students are prompted to do with it. Students could be required to engage and unpick the content in more detail in smaller groups, or to complete a task using the information;
- teachers need to be sensitive to students' attention levels. Exactly how long students can pay attention for depends on the individual, the topic (it's easier to focus on something interesting!) and the situation. As a rule, however, it's best to keep explanations short and snappy (as exemplified in Scenario 5.1, above);
- retaining the information depends on students' ability to integrate new learning with what they already knew (Wittrock, 1974). That is, do they have relevant schema knowledge? If they do, 'telling' can be a very efficient strategy

(Schwarz & Bransford, 1998). However, if a teacher is relatively unfamiliar with the learners, it would be helpful to take some time to figure out the levels of prior knowledge in the class (i.e., their starting point), to avoid some aspects of an explanation going 'over their heads';

- slides, worksheets or other visuals can make it easier for students to keep track of what they are listening to. For example, a flow chart could be shown, scaffolding the stages of a process or argument and show each section of learning within a context such as the formation of a business, or a scientific experiment;

- time needs to be allowed for consolidation. If a longer explanation is to be used, it could be broken up with one or more brief reflective tasks, or time allocated to taking notes. Rather than seeing a verbal explanation as the entire activity, it would be better to follow it up with a consolidation (immediately or after a delay) where learners have to summarise the information in their own words – a good and simple use of retrieval practice.

As mentioned above, we may have students in our lessons who need more support with understanding material, and students may have different prior knowledge. This is often apparent in English lessons where some students have more cultural awareness than others do, affecting their understanding of a text. For example, in the novel *The Lord of the Flies* by William Golding, the author expects the reader to understand themes such as a society without rules and regulations.

Telling, discussion or explaining things in several ways with examples will help students to understand the information better. We might use our deep knowledge of our class here to help us support individual students. Consider the example below (Scenario 5.2).

## SCENARIO 5.2

Mr P is a sociology teacher and is taking a class he hasn't worked with before. At the start, he gives the class explanation of the main theory covered in today's lesson and asks the students to take notes as he does so. However, he realises that some students look confused. He pauses, asks them to put their pens down and then engages in some questioning to gauge prior knowledge and starting points. He then explains part of the content more simply and briefly, asking learners to listen quietly, followed by setting the pupils a task to summarise what they have just heard in their own words. As they are doing so, Mr P circulates to check on what they are writing.

Overall, we probably can't get away from 'telling' as a strategy. It's simply too useful and flexible. All the same, as professionals, we should give some thought to how to make new ideas and information stick in the memory. This depends on prior knowledge, attention and processing, and on later consolidation. These considerations should form part of how we plan lessons.

## REFLECTION POINT

When planning lessons or schemes of learning, it might be worthwhile to consider the amount of teacher talk. Try asking 'what am I doing, what are they doing?' When planning to balance the amount of listening students have to do, consider ways of having the students actively engage with the content.

## STORYTELLING

A very specific example of *telling* comes when an educator tells their learners a story. Stories are naturally engaging; most learners stop and focus when a story begins.

If you don't think stories are relevant to your teaching context or subject, think again! Stories can be used with any age group and topic, and there is good evidence that a narrative approach is more effective than providing the same information without a narrative context. For example, when teaching about evolution, teachers may choose to present Darwin's voyages and discoveries in a dramatic, narrative way. There is evidence that such an approach is more memorable. Arya and Maul (2012) presented the same set of science information to middle school students either in a neutral way, or as a narrative which focused on a scientist's journey. The latter was significantly better remembered in a later test.

Overall, stories hack into many of the benefits discussed in the previous chapter. They have an in-built structure, making it easier for learners to keep track and mentally review the events – important for consolidation. The richly meaningful and sometimes emotion-heavy content makes them more memorable, too. The way that they focus on events from the perspective of a particular character makes them easier to relate to, especially for novice learners.

For educators who want to use stories, key points and principles for the classroom include:

- a story is distinguished from a general verbal explanation in that it has a narrative, characters and emotional stakes. These features make the experience of listening to a story feel less like an information dump;
- stories have many of the same pros and cons as verbal explanations; issues of attention and consolidation still apply. However, stories are easier for learners to follow (especially beginners);
- the key takeaways with a storytelling approach can nevertheless be obscure. Students may remember the story, but forget the point, or the key details. Care needs to be taken at the planning stages to ensure that opportunities to tease out this information are not lost in the activity of storytelling. A delayed quiz or similar retrieval-based task can help to arrest forgetting. Teacher questioning or plenary-type activities (see below) can also help to reinforce the key learning objectives from a story.

## VISUAL TOOLS

In the modern classroom, it's less common for verbal explanations or stories to be shared without any visuals. PowerPoint slides have become a default tool and, in their absence, teachers often make use of diagrams, demonstrations, sketches, tables and so forth. A good-quality video combines verbal explanations and visual stimuli in an especially rich and engaging way. In addition, there are many visual prompts available to students in the form of written notes, handouts, or textbooks which they can access both during the lesson and independently as part of home study.

While both visual and verbal information can be retained in long-term memory, there is some evidence that combining the two can lead to a better chance of new information being retained. This is known as dual coding (see also Chapter 3).

A curious issue here is that we know that working memory is limited, so it might be assumed that additional visual information will overload and distract learners. And, indeed, it appears that this can happen. So-called *seductive details* such as cartoons on slides can draw learners' attention away from the main point that the teacher is trying to get across (Swaffer, 2019).

However, a well-chosen diagram can really boost understanding. In part, this is because working memory can support both verbal and visual processing simultaneously (see Chapter 2), and visuals can therefore act as support while a learner is tackling a verbal task. For example, in religious studies, a teacher may use a diagram or slide showing the front of a church while verbally explaining to students the artefacts and the meaning behind them during a church service.

There are therefore professional choices to be made about what visuals to use. When done well, the provision of visual information can scaffold the learning that occurs via verbal explanations, but, when done poorly, these can be a distraction.

Videos, too, could vary in terms of whether the visual information is helpful or a hinderance to memory. Many videos – documentaries, for example – have a lot of visual information and audio. They are easy to follow, but the key information may be rapidly forgotten if it is not consolidated, just like with a verbal explanation alone (see above).

While note-taking can help, it's important again to consider the limits of working memory. Taking in information from a video and also writing notes on it is a form of multitasking, and learners could well miss information. For this reason, a teacher could instead ask learners to give videos their full attention and then pause after a few minutes so that the class can summarise the ideas from memory. This way, they are only completing one task at a time and the processing of the video content can be more focused and active.

For teachers who are using visuals, key points and principles for the classroom include:

- learners can process both visual and verbal information at once, but this depends on neither being overly complex;
- a well-chosen diagram can enhance understanding of a text, but it's best to minimise the use of decorative visuals that don't add to understanding. These may actually detract from learning;
- as with verbal explanations, information in a video can be rapidly forgotten, so immediate consolidation would be worthwhile – for example, via a plenary task or quiz (or both). Learners could also be asked to verbally summarise the main points immediately after watching a documentary or video clip;
- note-taking during a video is overly demanding on working memory, so it could be worthwhile to pause a video periodically so that students can take notes, or prompt them to do so at the end.

## REFLECTION POINT

How much time do you give learners to think about and summarise what they hear in an explanation or video? How quickly does the lesson move on? On the basis of what you have read, would it be worth giving learners a few minutes immediately after to summarise what they have heard in their own words?

## DEMONSTRATIONS

One specific example of a visual tool involves giving a demonstration. Consider examples such as the following:

- in chemistry, a teacher explains the correct set-up of the apparatus for an experiment to identify the ions in an ionic compound, using a Bunsen burner, nichrome wire, sodium chloride and hydrochloric acid;
- a food science teacher shows students how to bake bread, explaining the steps aloud;
- a physical education teacher explains the recommended footwork and movements to be used during bowling in cricket;
- a design technology teacher gives a safety briefing to their class before a woodwork task, showing the electric drill equipment that should be used and how to do this safely.

In each of the examples above, the teacher is not simply *telling* learners information. They are showing the steps at the same time. This combination of explanation and demonstration can be more effective and powerful, for two main reasons:

- it combines visual and verbal information (dual coding);
- the visuals can scaffold understanding, making the explanation easier to understand.

Whether this is viable or not may depend on the task. In some subjects, these approaches are already standard practice and should be continued. However, teachers should bear in mind the forgetting that will take place very soon after the demonstration or modelling. Many of the same considerations raised above still apply. Students may remember the gist of the demonstration, but get the details or the order of steps confused or mixed up.

Researchers in metacognition advocate using 'think aloud' procedures, and demonstrating thought processes with accurate terminology (e.g., EEF, 2018; Pintrich, 2002), so it is worth thinking about ways to use demonstrations more widely. A politics teacher could show how to craft the first paragraph of an essay, showing an example on screen and talking learners through the process. Some teachers use visualisers for 'live marking' of exam answers, to demonstrate to students what successful answers have done well. In computer science, a teacher might talk through the steps of a coding task before students begin to work on this independently.

Overall, key points and principles for the use of demonstrations include:

- memory considerations that apply to other educational formats still apply, including managing load on working memory, providing time for consolidation and prompting active retrieval of main points;
- teachers for whom demonstrations are regularly used should consider the impact of forgetting;
- teachers for whom demonstrations are *not* regularly used should consider ways that they could be incorporated in future.

## READING

Discussion of the value of visual information leads on to a consideration of *reading*. Like listening to a verbal explanation, reading is both important and ubiquitous across education. It is one of the oldest educational tools in the box.

However, textbooks are frequently seen as a bad thing and often are associated with leading to boring and ineffective lessons. We feel that this is quite a short-sighted attitude, particularly given that 'research on the internet' is such a widely used strategy by both students and teachers alike. Unlike the internet, most textbooks have gone through a process of rigorous quality control and they tend to have been written by experts (textbooks also contain a lot more than just text!). The internet also has some good resources, but it has plenty of bad and misleading ones too.

Granted, it's possible to teach a boring lesson that focuses on a textbook. However, textbooks can also be used in stimulating, creative and active ways. For example, in a history lesson about the United States' entry into World War II, a textbook chapter could be used as a resource and students could be asked to find and rank a list of main arguments based on their reading, giving reasons.

Of course, schools will often use on-screen materials, whether via a virtual learning environment, interactive whiteboards, or individual student devices. One consideration from the research is that on-screen reading is often done more rapidly by students, with a tendency to skim read that is not found with printed sources (Clinton-Lisell, 2019). As a consequence, on-screen materials are more poorly remembered. However, students often don't appreciate this difference, mistakenly thinking that they are learning better via an on-screen resource.

However, the format of the reading material itself, whether online or paper based, may be less important than what the teacher requires the learners to *do* with the information contained in it. For example, in the history lesson mentioned above, it doesn't matter if learners initially skim read the material, as long as they are later prompted to engage with it more deeply and to use the information.

Indeed, reading provides a very useful opportunity for learners to engage with the active learning strategies discussed earlier. It is not inherently passive and provides opportunities for learners to move at their own pace, to stop and think, and to check, re-read or summarise where necessary. Students may also engage more deeply with the reading task if they know it will be routinely followed up and the information will be used in some way afterwards.

It is often assumed that reading is a visual task. However, text that enters working memory is rapidly converted to sound (a good example of how separation between 'auditory learners' and 'visual learners' doesn't make psychological sense!). This means that learners can easily process visual information as well as written text – a diagram alongside an explanation, or a picture illustration in a children's book, for example.

As with some of the other strategies mentioned, reading relies on learners connecting what they read to prior knowledge. We should be aware that successful reading is not just about being able to decode a text (although that set of skills is a prerequisite), but also about having the knowledge to make sense of what the words mean. Although giving more time can help struggling readers to make sense of a text, in many contexts it will also be valuable for educators to consider learner starting points in advance of reading, and to pre-teach key concepts, key terms and vocabulary.

Overall, reading is a great way of developing new ideas and understanding in memory. Reading is an important skill in itself and, by engaging in it, learners are both practising this skill and improving their knowledge.

To sum up, key points and principles for the use of reading include:

- reading has many of the same advantages as a verbal explanation, but it allows learners to go at their own pace. This makes it easier for them to pause, reflect and connect new ideas to existing schemas. Planning can be done flexibly to account for this – for example, by allowing twenty minutes overall to both read a passage and to attempt core and extension questions;
- reading often (though not always) has a story element. Reading a novel or narrative non-fiction text can be more engaging and memorable, for the reasons mentioned in the previous section;
- it's easy to assume that poor reading is mainly due to reading skills, but the previous points about schemas suggest another issue – if learners lack the background knowledge to understand a text, then they will struggle to read it;

- it is perhaps unfair to describe reading as a passive task, but how active it is depends on what the reader is required to do. Teachers may ask students to find and report key facts, prompting learners to scan a text actively. Even free reading can be relatively active, but this depends on the reader and is hard to guarantee;
- for all the benefits of reading, it is more useful if there is an effective follow-up. Reading a text can be a good way to get information into the learner's mind, but this should typically be followed by actively using the information in some way, ideally incorporating retrieval practice activities (see Chapter 1). It is inefficient for learners to re-read the same text again and again as a study strategy (see Chapter 7 for more on study strategies!).

## ACTIVITY

To experience what it feels like to read a text when you don't have the background knowledge to process it, try reading the following sentence, taken from a news article: 'the specialist leg spinner led the attack in a white ball series dominated by seam'.

If this is hard for you to understand, it's because it's based on sports terminology. Understanding the words is not enough – reading also depends on having a well-developed schema (in this case, about cricket).

## ACTIVITY

To show how written words tend to be converted to sounds in your head, try showing a slide with random letters for a few seconds and then asking learners to write down what they can remember.

You will notice that mistakes that they make tend to be on the basis of letters that sound similar (e.g., B, D, P), rather than ones that look superficially similar (e.g., O and Q).

## QUESTIONING AND QUIZZES

It is well known to most teachers that questioning is an important aspect of classroom practice. However, we can also draw on memory principles to make it even more effective and to guide how best to do it.

First, let's briefly consider the formative assessment role of questioning. For many educators, this is the main reason to engage in questioning – checking what learners know and addressing gaps and misunderstandings in their growing knowledge. We support this because it helps teachers to target teaching where it is most needed.

However, what is sometimes neglected is the *retrieval* aspect of classroom questioning. Asking questions invites learners to access ideas from their LTM, thus engaging in retrieval practice. This will sometimes happen with formative questioning, but overall, it implies a different purpose and format of questioning. Questioning for retrieval practice is not about checking what learners know or identifying misconceptions, but rather about consolidating things that they have previously been taught.

Questioning that focuses on retrieval is best done on a whole-class basis – for example, via written quizzes or 'show me boards' (mini-whiteboards), for these ensure that everyone is retrieving things from memory, not just one pupil! These can also be used for follow-up questioning. For example, in a politics lesson, the teacher could ask learners to write down the three branches of the US government, then ask questions such as 'Which branch is responsible for making laws?'

If whiteboards are not available or not practical under the circumstances, then it can be helpful to use a 'cold calling' approach, where learners do not put their hands up, but the teacher instead calls out a name at random. If anyone can be asked, there is more emphasis on *every* learner to think about the correct response and try to have the answer ready (thereby retrieving it from memory, even if they don't say it out loud).

The success rate of retrieval-focused questioning should be higher than is (often) the case with formative questioning. After all, if learners fail to answer the question, they haven't benefited from retrieving the knowledge from memory. Rosenshine (2012) recommends aiming for an 80 per cent success rate when quizzing. Any easier, and the questions may be too easy (see also Chapter 6 for how the difficulty level might need be adapted for some learners).

Quiz questions are often best if they are planned carefully and tailored per class, based on the teacher's knowledge of that individual class. It's less useful to set a random set of ten questions from a prior topic. Instead, the questions should be sequenced and chosen as those which will cause the students a suitable level of challenge to support consolidation. It's also worth bearing in mind that success on a quiz can prompt learners to focus on the outcome – 'look how well I have scored' – leading to over-confidence and a false sense of secure learning.

Bear in mind that quiz questions are not just about factual recall but can also support higher-order skills. Here, the purpose is to deepen understanding. A mix of skills-based and fact-based retrieval questions is more effective in developing skills than consolidating facts alone (Agarwal, 2019).

Another memory consideration relevant to questioning is the spacing effect. When exactly do we ask questions of students? Common practice, arguably, is to do so during the lesson when the material was first taught. However, this does not lead to spaced practice. Part of our process of planning questions or quizzes should include re-using previous questions after a delay (which will also be more difficult, in line with previous points).

Pre-questioning is also an effective strategy. This is where learners encounter questions *prior* to studying the information. For example, perhaps history students are going to learn about the factors that led to World War I. Pre-questioning could include asking them about what events prompted the war, which country was allied with which, who invaded who, etc. Of course, most pupils will struggle to answer these questions before learning the topic! The point is not to get the answer right, or to assess understanding, but rather to have them think about and reflect on the question.

There is strong evidence that pre-questioning benefits learning. Why? One reason may be that it draws the attention of the student more to the content. If they have been asked, 'Which country invaded Serbia at the outset of the war?' and couldn't answer, then when they later learn that Austria-Hungary declared war on and invaded Serbia, it is more likely to grab their attention. And paying attention and being curious facilitates memory.

In some ways, then, pre-questioning functions rather like a learning intention, but is arguably more engaging and specific. Consider a learning intention like the following:

Today we are going to learn about the events that led to the start of World War I.

It's accurate, but not very specific ... or interesting! Learners may glaze over when presented with such a statement. They are likely to focus more on pre-questions like the following:

- whose assassination triggered World War I?
- which country invaded Serbia at the start of the war?
- which countries were allied with Germany?

Such questions help to generate learners' curiosity, as well as indicating what they need to learn from the lesson.

However, it may be important to reassure learners that they are not expected to know the answers at this stage; they will get to formulate the right answers as the lessons progress and they learn the material. This might take some getting used to for the class, but over time pre-questioning can play an important role in the lesson. And like other questions, it can serve a formative purpose, too.

Overall, then:

- questioning can play an important formative role, but it can also play a vital role in consolidation via retrieval practice;
- quizzes and other forms of questioning that stimulate every pupil to answer (or think about the answer) are preferable, and there should be a high but not perfect success rate in answering the questions;
- the spacing effect can be applied, using questions to consolidate material after a delay;
- pre-questioning is also an effective strategy. This involves asking questions prior to presenting new material in order to generate curiosity and focus attention.

## REFLECTION POINT

Think about two or three ways that you could apply these ideas to questioning in your context. Can you use more delayed practice in quizzes – for example, more whole-class questioning, or more pre-questioning?

## GROUPWORK

For the purposes of this section, we will define groupwork as any situation where two or more learners are working together on a task without their interactions being directly controlled and supervised by a teacher. A plenary is not a groupwork task by this definition, but 'think–pair–share' is.

When working in a pair or group, discussion is a key aspect of the learning situation. It provides opportunities for one learner to share what they know with others, and for learners to work creatively together to puzzle something out. For example, in a drama lesson a group may share ideas about how best to act out and present a performance to show key themes of a scene.

Working in a group is clearly going to be a practical necessity for certain subjects and tasks – musical performances, sports matches, language learning and science experiments all spring to mind. In other subjects, it may be more of a choice. And there are memory-related reasons why teachers may use this particular strategy.

Groupwork can support students in understanding concepts, and also to draw out misconceptions or misunderstandings. We have probably all been in a situation where a conversation helped us to understand something more clearly; this can happen in the classroom too. Think of debates, research groups, therapy sessions; there are many situations where learning is not just about getting information directly from another person but about discussing it with others.

Peer teaching is also an effective pedagogical strategy and is facilitated by group contexts. It can be a practical way for teachers to provide differentiated learning for those that are struggling, given that the teacher can't always help multiple pupils at once. And higher-attaining students also benefit from peer teaching because this forces them to think deeply about the material (and therefore involves deep processing) and to retrieve it from memory (retrieval practice). Lower-attaining students benefit from mixed-attainment groups too (e.g., Burris et al., 2008).

However, while groupwork can be a useful strategy, it shouldn't be the default. We would argue that, instead, groupwork should be used where it has clear advantages over direct teaching. For example, in computer science it would be clearer to show students how to write code to run on a loop, rather than have students discuss this in a group. The teacher is the expert in the subject, and sometimes it is simply much more efficient for them to explain how something works than have learners puzzle it out. Having said that, it can be useful for learners to *briefly* try something before getting an explanation from the teacher – for example, asking students to try the same code as above and asking them why certain steps happen at each stage and why the code may stop working. Doing so acts as a form of pre-questioning (see 'Questioning and Quizzes', above), helping them to understand the problem before hearing the solution.

Overall, balance needs to be struck between opportunities to explore ideas and the need for new information from the teacher. It's worth asking yourself – are your group tasks always time efficient? Clear instructions are also valuable to keep things focused.

Groupwork also has the potential for freeloading, where one or more learners do less than their peers. In line with everything that has been said about memory and learning so far, students are not going to be developing and consolidating their understanding if they are not taking in or using information and skills. It's critical to ensure that every learner is engaged in the learning task. For this reason, group size deserves some consideration. Teachers may want to aim for smaller groups on the whole, except in situations (such as brainstorming, perhaps) where the sharing of multiple perspectives and ideas are a key part of the task.

There is also a risk that the ideas which peers share are flawed or incorrect. In some circumstances, they may give their classmates bad advice and discussions could lead to confusion. Consider, for example, which would be better if students were preparing for the exam – a brief explanation of the exam format by the teacher, or a group discussion about exam format in which each learner shared what they had heard or assumed. Again, a discussion may act as a form of pre-questioning, but it should be kept quite short!

Overall, then, key points and principles for the use of groupwork include:

- groupwork can apply to any task being done by two or more pupils. It contrasts with direct instruction by the teacher. It is useful, but should not be the default strategy;
- groupwork can support understanding by letting learners think deeply about topics, or work out solutions using existing information. It can therefore support memory and learning;
- groupwork can allow learners to share ideas and experiences, but, likewise, there is a risk that they will share misconceptions and flawed information, especially as the teacher cannot be in all places at once in the classroom;
- overall, when groupwork is used, it may be useful to keep groups small, timings short, instructions clear and to used mixed-attainment groups where appropriate.

## REFLECTION POINT

For your teaching subject/area, take a few minutes to think about the optimal size of group. The more students in a group, the less time each of them will get to speak. Is that a problem? Are there situations where a larger group would be beneficial?

## PROJECT WORK

Project work is a broad category, which in our own experience as educators has ranged from young children pond dipping to older learners creating miniature satellites, coding 3D printers, or even running businesses.

There are two things that most projects have in common, though:

- they are to some extent self-directed, with learners working at their own pace;
- the steps towards a goal – and sometimes the goal itself – are not fully set out by the teacher in advance.

A project could be an individual or shared task. If it is a group project, many of the issues raised in the previous section will apply. In particular, they are a good opportunity for learners to think deeply about the topic, and share ideas.

If well chosen (perhaps with a degree of learner choice), projects can be highly motivating to learners and the value of that motivation can't be over-stated. Interest and enthusiasm are highly beneficial to memory. People remember things which are relevant to them (see Chapter 3) and to which they pay more attention. Just consider how much students can tell you about their personal hobbies and interests.

It's therefore worth thinking carefully about how to guide learners towards projects that will both harness their curiosity and passions, and consolidate key skills and factual information that has been learnt previously. For example, Scenario 5.3 shows how student interests can be linked to key syllabus ideas, striking a balance between interests and consolidation.

## SCENARIO 5.3

Mr S teaches psychology and asks his students to select individual projects based on their interests at the end of an introductory topic on perspectives in psychology. This allows students to pick an area that they find personally fascinating (serial killers is a popular choice), while consolidating the main psychological perspectives that have been taught earlier in the topic. It is made clear that the information students find on the topic must be analysed in terms of which perspective it supported, with at least two main perspectives forming the focus. For example, students can compare genetic and upbringing-based explanations for criminal behaviour.

There are a few other memory factors discussed earlier in this book that fit well with project work. A project is spaced out over time, potentially benefitting from the spacing effect. It typically involves active learning of some kind, and a high degree of focus and attention (fully occupying working memory). And it often culminates in some form of output, be it producing something, writing something, or giving a presentation. All of these outputs can further deepen understanding and prompt retrieval.

Even when learners struggle on a project, this can benefit memory. They may well get stuck at certain points, and have to figure out how to proceed via further research, or gain guidance from a peer or the teacher – a form of scaffolding.

However, for these things to be as effective as possible, the process needs to be set out in the right way. Some pre-teaching of relevant material needs to take place if learners are to later consolidate it and to benefit from spaced practice. They need to have developed certain tools and skills so that they know how to tackle problems that they face. And the conditions of the project work need to allow for focus and minimise distractions in working memory.

Some thought needs to also be given to what exactly learners will learn and consolidate. In a well-designed project, they will have opportunities to link up, deepen and add to prior learning. In a more poorly designed one, they may be forced to find out a lot of new information that is unconnected to prior and later lessons and which will be rapidly forgotten due to a lack of consolidation.

To sum up:

- project work can draw on a range of the memory-based benefits discussed elsewhere in this book; by being motivating it will be even more highly memorable;
- however, careful thought needs to be devoted to the planning of the project, ensuring that learners will be consolidating syllabus-relevant material under conditions that support successful learning.

### REFLECTION POINT

Think of a specific project that you regularly teach or that you are familiar with from your context. What concepts or theories are learners consolidating? Could more be done to pre-teach relevant information so that it is consolidated as they work on the project? And will there be some kind of follow-up (spaced practice) at a later point?

## CONCLUSION

What we have described in this chapter still only covers some of the activities and tasks that are used in classrooms. Hopefully, however, most of the important principles have been touched upon; by showing certain principles and how they connect to theories of memory, we hope that you can see how these could be combined and applied in creative new ways to suit your own context.

One of the great things about teaching is that we have so many options – no two classes are the same and every lesson could potentially be modified and refined to make it more stimulating and more memorable. In that process, it pays to be mindful of 'best bets'. That is to say, lots of strategies work, but some are more likely to be impactful than others.

Strategies that in some way draw on desirable difficulties such as retrieval practice or otherwise boost learning (rather than performance) will be preferable overall. However, we also need to consider how students respond when we make learning more challenging by doing things like varying the context or delaying practice. Such tasks will, inevitably, feel a little more difficult for students and they will need to be prepared for this beforehand. And for some learners that may be threatening or anxiety-provoking.

The next chapter will explore this issue in more depth, considering variations in student memory, as well as some of the ways that strategies can be adapted or differentiated to ensure that they remain both appropriate and effective.

## KEY POINTS

- Memory principles can be applied to every type of classroom tasks, from teacher explanations to project work.
- By drawing on the science of learning and on an understanding of memory in particular, we can format our lessons in ways that are familiar to us and the students but make these tasks more effective.
- Tasks that involve new input – explanations, reading and so forth – benefit from active learning strategies and students having the time and opportunity to consolidate the material and link it to what they already know.
- There are various reasons for using questioning and we should think broadly; the strategy is not just about formative assessment but can also play a role in consolidation – pre-questioning makes learners more receptive to later information.
- Tasks such as groupwork and project work can provide opportunities for consolidation and deepening of knowledge, but care needs to be taken over how these are set up in order to ensure that time is spent effectively.

# 6

# WHY DO STUDENTS DIFFER IN MEMORY, SKILL AND ATTAINMENT?

## INTRODUCTION

Much of the discussion about memory so far in this book has focused on principles which are applicable to all learners. In this chapter, we will focus on issues that are specific to the individual. For example, how can some of the desirable difficulties – such as spacing – be modified for struggling students? Do some students really have a 'bad memory' causing them to forget to do homework? We will discuss the common areas where teachers may see their students struggling, and identify common challenges and possible solutions.

Throughout this book, we have explored some of the major principles of memory that underpin learning. In doing so, we have made numerous suggestions and recommendations for practice, focusing on things that are 'good bets', and that can make tasks more effective within the limited teaching time we have. However, classrooms are diverse. Some learners understand and recall things more easily than others. It therefore makes sense to consider not just the tasks themselves, but also the way they might be tailored to the needs of the individual.

One obvious aspect is to consider whether desirable difficulties (see Chapter 3) are always desirable! For learners who find their courses/topics a struggle, could it be the case that there are already enough difficulties in the classroom, without us adding more? And how do we differentiate effectively, in a way that fits with the principles explained so far? After all, some differentiation strategies involve making things easier for learners, a fact that may appear to conflict with the concept of desirable difficulties.

First, though, let's consider a more widespread idea, something that most learners will say at some point or another: the idea that some people are forgetful or have a bad memory.

## PROSPECTIVE MEMORY

Teachers and students may talk about particular individuals as having a 'bad memory'. Some forget to do homework, fail to bring books or other items to class, or fail to show up to meetings as arranged. So, what light can the science of memory shine on this situation, and what can be done to support this?

To answer these questions, it is worth considering another aspect of memory that we haven't discussed so far: prospective memory. Prospective memory means remembering to do a particular task at a particular time in the future. For example, remembering to attend a pre-arranged meeting, return a phone call or complete a task later on in the day.

Prospective memory is quite challenging for any learner, but especially for younger ones. It is not really a separate memory 'store', but rather a system that draws on both long-term and working memory.

- Long-term memory is important because the task (appointment, duty, etc.) must be retained from the time the individual first learns about it until the moment that it becomes relevant. For example, if you tell a student in the morning that they should see the headteacher after the end of the school day, they must retain this in their LTM for several hours.
- Attention, working memory and executive functions are important because they are involved in monitoring what a learner is doing at a particular moment, and noticing if something important has been missed (for example, following from the example above, it's now the end of the school day and you are not outside the headteacher's office!).

There has been a great deal of research on prospective memory, although a lot of it involves rather artificial laboratory-based studies. Nevertheless, a few principles can be helpful to the classroom:

- unsurprisingly, external cues – for example, alarms, notes, or other physical reminders – can be important for attracting the individual's attention towards the task;
- tasks that prompt learners to think about cues will make them more likely to notice a relevant cue (Maylor, 1996);
- entering a 'flow state', while helpful and desirable in many respects, can lead to a situation where time seems to pass rapidly without the learner paying much attention to their external surroundings. Consequently, it can lead to individuals losing track of time;
- being in a routine, while once again helpful in some respects, can make it less likely that learners stop to evaluate their choices. Things that disrupt a routine can make it less likely that they will forget to do tasks.

Overall, these points suggest that students who have a 'bad memory' are not lacking in either working memory or long-term memory capacity. They may be no more likely to forget facts or skills than anyone else. Instead, their forgetfulness relates more to their habits and routines.

We can be mindful of this in terms of how to support students. Certain simple strategies can be used in situations where forgetting of tasks has become a problem:

- on a metacognitive level, reassure students that this is not a problem with their memory. This may help to boost their self-efficacy;
- identify problems specifically. For example, rather than taking about someone having a bad memory, you might try to pinpoint which things are most commonly being forgotten (for example, homework, meetings or whatever it may be);
- try to establish the points in the school day, or weekend, when the individual wants to do something but often forgets to do so;
- find ways of disrupting their routine at that point, so that they are prompted to consider what they should do less automatically;
- failing this, develop systems of specific reminders, such as alarms on a mobile phone or other device.

Of course, some pupils may use the idea of having a bad memory as an excuse for not completing homework or other tasks. Being informed about prospective memory and having a set of strategies to tackle it may discourage students from this!

## REFLECTION POINT

Do you have experience of being forgetful or missing appointments? Did it happen at particular times, or connected with particular types of activities? Can you think of any strategies that you successfully used in the past to improve your prospective memory?

# HELPING LEARNERS TO BETTER APPRECIATE HOW LEARNING WORKS

The points raised about tackling students' views about having a bad memory raise a broader point – students will often have pre-formed beliefs about the effectiveness of their own memory, or their capacity as a learner. And these may be out of sync with reality.

Learners may think that they are bad at a particular type of school subject (reading, science and maths being popular examples), failing to recognise the important role of practice. As the theories of LTM and schemas discussed so far in this book suggest, memory is not in any way fixed. Some people may find it harder to take in new information, but the more you know, the easier it is to take in and expand your knowledge further. Having a foundation of well-developed knowledge is the best way to ensure you are ready to learn more on the same topic. This is why the best curricula have a clear sequence and coherence, ensuring that the basics have been covered thoroughly before learners have to tackle the next idea sequentially (Crehan, 2018).

These points may remind you of the concept of mindset as discussed by Carol Dweck and others (e.g., Dweck, 2006). A fixed mindset, according to this perspective, is the belief that ability is relatively fixed, and a growth mindset is the belief that ability can change. Memory theory fits well with that idea. It's important for learners to realise that they have the capacity to improve and that ability is not fixed, as it will encourage them to take steps to develop their knowledge and to study effectively.

A student's outside interests provide a great analogy for how learning is cumulative and open to practice. Consider how you learn chess, a new sport, or a new computer game. It's easy to see that this is a process – you don't become good overnight. It's also easy to see that skill depends a lot on putting in the hours of practice (though perhaps a bit harder to see how the efficacy of that practice makes a difference).

These hobbies and activities – many of which take place in school clubs – provide a very different discourse to that which is often present in formal education. How often do you hear people say that some children are 'just not A-grade kids', or otherwise imply that some learners are incapable of a top grade? Such messages are out of touch with the role that memory and practice play. In school, as with games and hobbies, you only become competent by putting in the time and effort. And following the message throughout this book, think how much more impact those hours of practice will have if the practice is done in an effective way – a way that is active, meaningful, spaced out over time and that supports consolidation in long-term memory?

When learning is sufficiently challenging, students should struggle to grasp things the first time, and we as teachers need to recognise this and plan for it. This will slow down classroom teaching, but the longer-term gains are better than rushing through the content. We will explore strategies for doing this later in this chapter.

## INDIVIDUAL NEEDS AND THE BRAIN

Next, let's address a more fundamental concern for many teachers – the idea that some learners have lower ability, limited working memory, or some other processing difficulty. These concepts can be explained in terms of memory, leading to implications for what teachers should seek to do to support certain learners.

Working memory (WM) is the part of the mind that is involved in a great deal of thinking and processing in the here-and-now, including problem solving (see Chapter 2). It therefore plays a central role in hundreds of learning-related activities. At its most basic level, WM is involved in taking in and processing information over very brief timescales (less than a minute). For example, it processes the language we hear if a teacher speaks in French about how to order from a menu, or when students are copying text from a slide about velocity in physics.

The central executive part of the working memory model is also the basis of a set of abilities known as 'executive functions' – so called because they involve controlling many of our other actions and decisions. These executive functions include staying on task, monitoring how a task is going, and task switching where needed. As with working memory more broadly, such capacities are vitally important to functioning in formal education (Diamond, 2013).

Researchers don't entirely agree on whether to see executive functions as a part of working memory or as a system that controls working memory. For the teacher, the key point is that executive functions control many of the things that students do when working on a task.

There is general agreement that the frontal lobe of the brain is responsible for working memory and for executive function, and that this brain area develops quite slowly. In fact, it is still developing well after students leave secondary school. We can expect to see such abilities improve with age.

However, regardless of their age, some students experience difficulties of various kinds with their working memory or other related capacities. Clearly, given the points made above, such pupils are going to find some aspects of learning very challenging, and find themselves at a disadvantage compared to their peers. The specific challenges that they face may be very numerous and widespread, simply because working memory and executive functions are involved in so many tasks.

As scientists understand a lot about the parts of the brain involved in WM and executive function, we know that there is probably a neural basis to some such problems. This book is not about neuroscience, and it is beyond the scope of the book to delve into the causes of specific difficulties. We will instead focus on potential classroom *solutions*.

However, there are a couple of basic observations we can make before moving on to those solutions:

- first, there can be little doubt that many of the cognitive problems we observe among students started from an early age, and some may have a genetic component. It is important to make adjustments and to provide tailored support to certain learners, such as those with autism, dyslexia and many other differences or needs;
- second, the human brain is malleable. Neural plasticity means that brains change their structure in response to experience. This is especially the case when we are young. For school students, a lot of progress can be made in overcoming difficulties when the right support and opportunities for practice are in place;
- third, this argument is not meant to diminish or undermine the idea of neurodivergence. The young people in school classrooms are neurodiverse, and the goal is not to make them more homogeneous. Rather, whether students have additional needs or not, the aspiration is to support them in learning, and to help them achieve the skills and knowledge that will help them to achieve their own goals and otherwise equip them for life.

Overall, this presents quite a positive message for educators to embrace and share. Learners are different in multiple ways, many of them face great challenges, but the good news is that all of them can improve.

## ACTIVITY

Neuroscience is a broad and fast-moving field. While it's not always directly applicable to the classroom, there are findings that provide fascinating insights into learning and behaviour. Why not start up a discussion group with colleagues about this, and share some recent articles? Alternatively, this could be a regular topic for an ongoing staff professional learning group.

## SUPPORT AND DIFFERENTIATION

Differentiation means providing support for some students that differs from what is provided for the majority. Given how memory underpins learning, our understanding of memory can inform how we apply this support.

Linking back to the explanation of WM from Chapter 2, you will perhaps remember three key ideas or theories:

- the idea of cognitive load: each individual learner can only process a certain amount of information at any one time;
- the idea of a multi-part working memory system;
- the idea that working memory is supported by long-term memory. More knowledge makes thinking and processing easier.

Without getting into the debate over which theory of working memory is best, each of these ideas can imply some fairly uncontroversial ideas for practice. And whether or not they look at working memory as the first stage of memory or as something more integrated with LTM, most cognition researchers agree that working memory is very limited in its capacity. It makes sense not to expect students to process more than a few items at a time.

There is also broad agreement that working memory capacity varies across individuals and develops with age. We can expect to see a gradual increase in learners' ability to do very WM-demanding tasks – for example, to retain a sentence for a few seconds, or to multitask. But given that even adults find these things hard, it makes sense at any stage not to tax learners' working memory beyond what they can cope with, especially when they are faced with new skills or complex sets of information. As well as being a poor way to present a task, information overload may also cause them to feel stressed.

It may be useful as a classroom teacher to consider students as having different memory 'ages' in the classroom, ranging from those with particular support needs through to the more capable. However, it is also worth noting that such factors are open to change over time. To meet student needs, it is vital to get to know them on an individual level and to gauge their progress.

Incoming information is often going to be too much for learners if it all comes at once. Teachers therefore need to consider the pace of information (see points about videos and verbal presentations in the previous chapter, Chapter 5), allowing learners more time to process and consolidate things if necessary.

Many well-meaning approaches to active learning add to cognitive load without focusing on deepening knowledge and understanding. For differentiation to be effective, it is essential that a task remains focused on the learning objective, albeit in a way that is supported or scaffolded. For example, if a learner is supposed to be multiplying fractions, then simply tracing around the numbers on a sum that is already completed would not constitute helpful differentiation, as it neither involves doing the target skill nor working towards it. As Francis et al. (2018) explain, rather than teaching to the 'middle', we can aim high, and think about what support some learners need to achieve the objectives.

Learners will also find information more taxing to manipulate when it is new to them. For example, imagine a business studies lesson where students are required to learn how to construct a full profit and loss account having only just studied the key terms (for example, revenue, cost of sales, liabilities, gross profit, etc.). Manipulating this new information is demanding. The teacher will want learners to be able to use the information in the profit and loss account to suggest strategies or future actions a business may take to increase their profit over time, but the basic information of knowing what each of the concepts means fully occupies their WM. To get around this problem, a scheme of learning may be planned where students initially practise only the three elements from the top half of the account: revenue, cost of sales and gross profit. Once their understanding of these terms is secure and students can use these concepts to calculate the gross profit, they can then move on to the second half of the account and, finally, to putting these together and tackling realistic scenarios.

# AVOIDING OVERLOADING STUDENTS

Overall, it remains the case that some students will be overloaded much faster than others due to individual differences. To an extent, then, this aspect of practice is about getting to know your students' individual capabilities and allowing for this when planning.

Don't overcomplicate the lesson with too many new concepts at once, as shown in the example of the profit and loss account in a business studies lesson above. Clarity about the aims of each individual lesson can help with this planning process. In addition, it can be valuable to think about removing excessive content from lessons and schemes of learning. In this sense, less is more; other ideas could be allocated to another lesson or left out completely.

Similarly, aim to remove unnecessary slides, images, words and 'teacher talk' (see Chapter 5). Limit distractions, use modelling of concepts and break down steps clearly. Plan for deliberate practice (see Chapter 8) on their own so students can see their own progress and learning being embedded, not in group work or as a team.

Other ways to avoid overloading students include giving clear examples, activating schemas before a task and practising keys words and vocabulary. Don't leave students to 'figure it out' for themselves.

# THE ROLE OF IMAGES

Learners can benefit from the use of carefully deployed visuals to support the processing of verbal information in working memory, too. There is strong evidence that visual and verbal information can be processed separately in working memory (e.g., Mayer, 2003), allowing one to support the other. This means that students are able to retain and process information in the working memory better when it is presented in a dual format.

There are many ways that visuals could be used to support the presentation of verbal information and manage cognitive load. These include:

- flow charts to support processes – for example, to show the steps to writing a simple computer code program;
- charts, graphs and other diagrams to support factual information or processes – for example, a diagram of the different types of cloud in geography;

- Venn diagrams or tables to support categorisation;
- images to support stories and examples;
- maps supporting an understanding of geographical processes or historical events.

However, as discussed in Chapter 5, it is important that images are relevant to the ideas being taught, otherwise they can act as a distraction rather than supporting learners. In addition, active learning principles still apply here. Visual diagrams may be better, but it is better still if students engage with these actively using strategies such as retrieval, as is the case in Scenario 6.1.

## SCENARIO 6.1

Mx N teaches biology and is preparing a lesson that focuses on the terminology for organelles of cells. They are aware that some of their students find the details hard to remember. However, it is also a very visual area. Since Mx N knows that students might forget diagrams that they passively look at in their textbook, they instruct their class to close all textbooks and discuss the diagram with a partner. The class are then asked to draw the diagram from memory. Finally, students are asked to check the original diagram, to check that they got the layout and terminology correct, making corrections where required.

## RECOMMENDED SUPPORT STRATEGIES

Drawing on the ideas discussed in this chapter so far, we can make certain general recommendations for differentiation techniques (we will add to these after saying more about LTM and differentiation later in this chapter). Broadly, differentiation should retain a focus on the target skill or concept, but in a way that reduces the demands on working memory or executive function. Approaches could include:

- reducing the number of elements in a task (element interactivity contributes to cognitive load). Ensure that tasks are broken down into a manageable number of steps and new information, with plenty of opportunity to practise, before introducing further content;
- providing a source of visual support, such as a diagram or flow chart (see 'The Role of Images' above);
- allowing the learner more time to work on the task – avoid moving on until students have demonstrated they have understood new material;

- removing extraneous details or examples, and reducing or eliminating decorative 'extras';
- allowing the learner to look at some aspects of the task in advance of class. This could include flipped learning, where students do some work beforehand. In an art lesson, students could practise different types of shading before having to use them in a class task;
- break some tasks down into more steps. For example, in a PE lesson that focuses on a complex dance routine, each section could be divided into smaller steps.

It is a good idea to have a range of scaffolding activities available for each lesson, to support pupils until they can complete the task independently. Once designed, they can be adapted and used again with other classes.

Another form of scaffolding focuses more on long-term memory. If a student doesn't have the necessary schema(s) to cope with a task, it will be more challenging. Solving this problem is not straightforward or quick, but some gaps in prior knowledge can be assessed and tackled through checking with a class what they know about a particular topic before starting to teach it. As well as gaps in knowledge, they may harbour misconceptions. For example, a primary class learning about the Roman Empire may have some knowledge and assumptions, but it is worth checking these before starting a unit of learning about the Romans and their society.

It's also worth bearing in mind that some tasks are to an extent 'self-differentiating' in that different students will engage with them in different ways. For example, students will work at different paces on a written task or a project. This is true of many open-ended tasks; such tasks can be set as extensions, making it easier for the teacher to manage timings when working with more diverse groups.

## THE ROLE OF ADDITIONAL SUPPORT TEACHERS

Whatever support strategies are used, it is well worth discussing the differentiation with an additional support teacher or teaching assistant where available. Where students are receiving extra support, these colleagues may be able to advise on how well they have coped in other classes, and which type of differentiation they tend to respond well to.

Teaching assistants are also experienced at adapting tasks in ways which are tailored to the needs of the students they are supporting. Their knowledge to support the classroom teacher cannot be underestimated. Consider discussing issues around memory with any colleagues who support your classes, too. They may have valuable insights to share; together you can develop a professional learning community which better understands the role of memory in learning and its relevance to differentiation specifically.

For many students, supporting strategies will only be there for scaffolding. As the learners grow in confidence with the material and the relevant skills, they may cease to need additional support, becoming able to work confidently with more complex sets of material. In other cases, a student's working memory deficits may link to more or less permanent disabilities, for which the use of support strategies will remain appropriate over the long term. If this is hard to judge for a specific pupil, it would be best to get advice from an educational psychologist, or an additional support lead/SENDCO in your setting.

## EXTENSION AND CHALLENGE

Differentiation is not just about supporting struggling students; it may, at times, be helpful to find ways to increase the level of challenge for those who are finding tasks quite easy. This is especially the case in classes which are academically diverse – for example, many primary classes or optional subjects in secondary schools. Extending and challenging high-attaining students will also provide time for their peers to consolidate core material.

For these students, a similar principle still applies – means of extending them should not detract from a focus on the skill or concept that is the focus on the lesson. However, you could add to this, asking such students to provide more or deeper examples and analysis, or to make links beyond the concept at hand. For example, in a lesson where students are asked to talk about the causes of the Vietnam War, those who require extension could be asked to draw comparisons with other historical conflicts that they have read about.

Some other ideas for extension that fit well with theories of memory and cognition include:

- reducing scaffolding more rapidly, allowing learners to show what they can do without support;
- increasing the extent to which learners are expected to independently plan and reflect on their own work – for example, in an art lesson, allowing students to choose independently which materials and methods to use when creating a collage, rather than directing them step by step;

- putting learners into smaller groups – for example, a pair – when other learners can divide work among three or four group members. This means knowing your class well and being able to pair the strongest students together!
- modifying the difficulty of quiz tasks – for example, in a chemistry lesson with multiple-choice quiz questions, additional 'distractor' options could be offered, compelling students to think about subtle differences between concepts.

Just as with differentiation for struggling learners, modifications should not take the focus away from the main aim of the task or lesson. Care should also be taken to avoid having students feel overwhelmed. A gradual ramping up of difficulty can prove best.

It is also worth bearing in mind whether extension tasks provide opportunities for stronger students that are never provided to others. For this reason, it's probably best if retrieval-type tasks are not used as extension. It would be best if *all* students engage in retrieval, not just those who are already attaining highly. Doing the latter may lead to a 'Matthew effect' – where a small gap between strong and weak grows gradually larger over time. Likewise, in English lessons or others where reading could be provided as an extension, there is a risk that only a subset of students is set extra reading, and that any gap in the class's reading skills (and, perhaps, their knowledge) will widen over time.

## ACTIVITY

Take a few minutes to reflect on your favourite 'go-to' differentiation strategies. Write each one down as a heading in a notebook. Now, jot down relevant memory concepts under each one. These could be ideas that support the strategy, ideas that go against it, or just things that you may need to consider more carefully. This is a task that you can return to regularly as your professional knowledge of memory builds.

## INDIVIDUAL NEEDS AND DESIRABLE DIFFICULTIES

From what has been said so far, it should be clear that differentiation shouldn't detract from the purpose of a task, or from the application of effective learning strategies. And some of the most effective learning strategies are those known as desirable difficulties. These make learning more effortful but are useful (desirable) because they make forgetting less likely, and help to ensure that what is practised is both retained and can be used flexibly in future.

However, could it be the case that for some learners, there are already enough difficulties in the classroom, without adding more? After all, the level of difficulty involved might be expected to vary among learners. What one learner finds quite difficult may be impossibly challenging for another, perhaps leading them to give up entirely. In short, we need to consider how to ensure that desirable difficulties are always desirable! 'If a learner does not have the background knowledge or skills to respond successfully to a given difficulty, it becomes an undesirable difficulty' (Bjork, 2018, p. 147).

First, let's briefly recap the desirable difficulties (see Chapter 3 for a fuller explanation) and why they work. Desirable difficulties increase challenge in a way that is useful and pedagogically appropriate. Examples of strategies that fall into this category include retrieval or self-testing, spacing out practice, variation in practice, self-explanation when reading notes, and interleaving. These factors make classroom tasks such as reading, discussions and project work more effective, but in the process, the tasks become subjectively harder, and students tend to make more errors.

The reason that these strategies work so well is because they mimic real life. In other words, the more similar we make the learning/practice situation to the real thing, the better information and skills can be retained and later used (Bjork, 2018). A greater correspondence between the practice situation and later use makes it easier for learners to transfer what has been learnt.

We should therefore ensure that these things are used for all learners, and they can be used straight away and at all ages. There isn't a group of pupils for whom being able to retain and apply what they study over the long term is unimportant! We shouldn't see these strategies as dispensable, able to be dropped if students are finding things too challenging. What can be changed is the level of challenge, and this is surprisingly straightforward. However, it is best tackled one strategy at a time.

## RETRIEVAL PRACTICE

In general, researchers recommend that students should be getting a success rate of around 80 per cent when trying to retrieve prior learning (Rosenshine, 2012). So, for example, you might aim to pitch the quiz at a difficulty level that means most learners are getting a few answers wrong.

The way to adjust this for struggling learners is not to dispose of the quiz entirely, but to modify the difficulty level for different students, while ensuring that all are still prompted to retrieve. Some modifications could include:

- providing hints and cues, such as an additional sentence reminding them of a previous example;
- reducing the number of wrong choices on a multiple-choice quiz;
- giving the entire quiz a little sooner to these pupils than to the rest of the class (though ideally, it should still not be given straight away).

Less helpful modifications include anything that means the learner is not retrieving things from memory. Don't have them work with a partner who will recall the answers, for example, and don't turn a retrieval task into a copy-the-answers task.

## SPACING

Spacing out practice is hard, but also effective. As teachers, we can bear in mind that the more time that has passed, the more our learners will have forgotten. We can also try to judge (using prior experience) how much forgetting of a topic is likely to have occurred. Researchers recommend that educators schedule review tasks for a point in time when learners are *on the verge of forgetting* but have not yet completely forgotten. To put it another way, a little bit of forgetting is useful, but we shouldn't leave it too long. Revisiting learning should be planned and factored in as part of a unit of learning.

The speed of forgetting will depend not just on the material, but on the learner. Those with less well-developed schemas, or who practised less effectively the first time the material was studied, will forget more rapidly. As the teacher, you can experiment with scheduling practice at different times for different learners.

## VARIED PRACTICE

Varied practice can happen in a number of ways, but some of the most straightforward include varying the format of the task, the context, or the place where practice takes place. Asking physics learners to write a short essay explaining particles instead of completing their usual practice problems is an example of varying the task. Studying outside instead of indoors is varying the location. For example, taking students to a local seaside as part of geography lesson to measure 'shore drift' for themselves, rather than seeing a short video of the process (this example is active, as well as varied).

The level of variation can range from high to low. For struggling learners, variation can be considered a bit like the 'spiciness' level of food – it can be stronger or weaker according to what is needed. For example, it would be easier to transfer what has been learnt about vectors from one written task to another, and harder to transfer the same principles to a real scenario involving plane travel.

In situations where it is impractical to vary things in different ways for different learners (for example, where the whole class is going to practice something outside), we can help struggling learners to cope with the difficulties by providing hints and reminders.

## SELF-EXPLANATION WHEN READING NOTES

Self-explanation is in some ways one of the easiest desirable difficulties to use, as it can be applied to the forms of study and practice that a lot of learners tend to choose. Many of them prefer to study from notes or do practice problems, and could be prompted to self explain.

The problem here lies in that some of the learners who would benefit most from this technique will tend to avoid doing it spontaneously, in part because struggling learners often lack awareness of their own weaknesses. They mistakenly think that their study habits are more effective than they are.

Again, it is not helpful to avoid the desirable difficulty, but rather to find ways to provide support:

- learners could be encouraged to use Cornell notes, a format which includes a box where they write a summary at a later date (see Chapter 7 for an explanation);
- this summary box could feature self-explanation prompts, for example. Explain what insights this provides, and how it links to what you knew before;
- if they find it too hard to figure out which terms to self-explain, these could be highlighted in their notes by the teacher.

## INTERLEAVING

Interleaving (see Chapter 4) has been used across a range of learning situations, including with very young children and the elderly. In addition, the underlying principle – inductive learning via categorising similar and different types of item – is a process that even young babies go through when they are first learning about the world.

For that reason, there is certainly no reason to avoid interleaving with struggling learners. They may in fact find it a more straightforward and intuitive way to learn than more 'direct teaching' approaches, in part because it involves learning via examples.

All the same, interleaving can be demanding on working memory because learners have to retain multiple examples or categories. Ways to manage this difficulty might include:

- showing fewer categories at a time – for example, if you were using interleaving to teach types of lake in geography, just two or three types of lake could be shown at a time;
- showing examples at the same time (e.g., on the same slide) rather than one after another (e.g., on two different slides spaced apart), making comparisons less demanding of working memory;
- making the similarities and differences between examples a little more obvious by giving hints such as by asking 'What difference in shape is there between these example lakes?'

A common theme for all of these strategies is that the level has to be appropriate. By making learning more challenging, it makes the practice situation more like the circumstances when learning is used in real life – and this has genuine benefits. Too difficult, and some of these benefits can be lost.

Overall, it's worth bearing in mind that these techniques work with all ability levels. Most have been demonstrated in the learning of pre-school children and even animals. Therefore, school students can cope with them in some form. The key is to ensure that the difficulty level is appropriate.

Bear in mind also that when difficulties are combined – for example, applying both spacing and retrieval to a revision activity – doing so will make things extra challenging. If it is hard to repeat a task after a delay, it will be even harder to do a quiz on it after a delay! For this reason, additional support and modifications may be needed in such cases, even for stronger and more confident students.

## SCENARIO 6.2

Mrs R, a business studies teacher, is aware that many students will struggle with the idea of current and long-term liabilities and fixed and current assets when working on calculating a balance sheet. To introduce this topic, Mrs R explores the concept of a wage of £1,500 coming into the family home at the end of the month and asks the students to list what the wage is 'exchanged' for over a period of time, For example, we may exchange some of the wage to pay for our mortgage/rent, we buy food and pay our bills and we

*(Continued)*

may save a small amount in our bank account as savings. We still have £1,500 at the end of the month, but it is no longer there in cash; it can still be accounted for, however. Similarly, a business brings in revenue and uses this revenue to buy assets, pay bills and may save some as cash to use for emergencies. We can see what the business owns and what it owes through the balance sheet. In using the example of the wage and how it is exchanged for other items, the students can relate this familiar concept to a business which may be more abstract to them.

## CONCLUSION

While theories of memory explain its stores and processes in generic ways, there are, of course, considerable individual differences among our students. In this chapter, we have seen that memory principles can underpin effective, evidence-based differentiation. Support strategies can focus on scaffolding learning, managing cognitive load and building schemas ahead of tasks. Memory principles can also inform effective challenge for our strongest students.

Desirable difficulties such as spacing and variation won't be experienced equally by all students. They can even become undesirable under some circumstances. We have now explored some of the ways that these can be modified, ensuring that the focus remains on the learning goals of the task, and does not undermine the essential process that makes the desirable difficulty effective.

### KEY POINTS

- Most classroom issues are not due to students having a 'bad memory'. The process known as prospective memory helps us to better understand why things are forgotten, and how to tackle this.
- Cognitive development is partly limited by the development of the brain, and working memory capacity varies across different students. This leads to a need for support. Overloading working memory is a risk, and planning should account for the need to take information in gradually, and to practise and consolidate before moving on.
- Support strategies could use images and diagrams, as these are processed by a different working memory store than verbal information.

- For students who would benefit from extension, tasks could ask for the generation of further examples or could increase difficulty. Care should be taken that other learners are not missing out.
- Desirable difficulties will vary in their level of challenge depending on factors such as a learner's prior knowledge and how rapidly they are likely to forget. This should be borne in mind, and difficulty varied where possible in order to make tasks more effective.

# 7

# MNEMONICS

## INTRODUCTION

We now discuss how memory processes and systems can be directly applied to some of the independent challenges that students face. Foremost among these challenges is students' need to learn curriculum content, so that they retain and can use it over the longer term.

Whether we like the role of exams in the education system or not, most learners need to sit multiple exams. As educators, we want them to pass these exams and pass them well. We also want to ensure that relevant knowledge is not forgotten after the exam, but retained so that it can be used skilfully in the future in relevant situations (i.e., that it can be *transferred*).

As discussed in Chapter 1, memory is not just about cramming for tests, but underpins group discussions, project work or the use of higher-order skills. Indeed, the kind of study tasks that students face when preparing for exams often represent a rather unnatural use of human memory. This is why it often feels so difficult. There is no doubt that memory retains some types of information more easily than others (e.g., Nairne et al., 2007) and that we tend to struggle to remember arbitrary details such as names and numbers, or the order of lists. Each learner is faced with a vast amount of knowledge, some of which feels confusingly abstract at first.

This chapter focuses on the mnemonics that can be applied to such situations, explaining how such techniques need not just be a tool for memorisation, but rather the beginning of a longer process that can support lasting learning. We explore the role of mnemonics in tackling complex material, consider how these techniques both illustrate and add to broader memory concepts covered so far, and then look at how some of the ideas behind mnemonics can be applied to the classroom and to other areas of education.

**REFLECTION POINT**

When was the first time you did a test or exam at school? How old were you and what was the topic? Did you know how to study effectively?

# WHAT ARE MNEMONICS?

A mnemonic means a memory technique – something that is used to support memory, usually when something would otherwise be very hard to retain. Some of the most famous examples include using phrases and rhymes to remember the order of the months of the year or the colours of the rainbow.

There are, in fact, multiple different types of mnemonic. All can be powerful if used appropriately, and they also illustrate different aspects of how memory stores work. Let's go through some of the most relevant ones one at a time.

## ACROSTIC PHRASES AND KEYWORD ACROSTICS

An *acrostic phrase* is where the first letter (or letters) of each word used can be combined to spell out a term. They are very useful for hard-to-remember new terminology and for lists where the order is important. Often, students will know and understand conceptual ideas but still forget important details, such as the order of a set (especially when this is fairly arbitrary, such as which month comes before which). An acrostic supports their memory for such details.

A good example is the use of an acrostic phrase to remember the order (in terms of wavelength and frequency) of the waves on the electromagnetic spectrum. Various such phrases are used by students and teachers; one example is as follows:

Raging Martians Invade Venus Using X-Ray Guns
(radio waves, microwaves, infrared, visible light, ultraviolet, x-rays, gamma rays).

Another, used to teach the correct order of financial documents, is as follows:

Pink Dragons Go In Red Coloured Sandcastles
(purchase order, delivery note, goods received note, invoice, receipt, credit note, statement of account).

It's important to bear in mind that such tools merely *support* learning, rather than being the end goal. When they have learnt the simple phrase, learners can use it as a cue for retrieval, thus supporting their developing conceptual understanding by helping to remind them that (for example) gamma rays have a shorter wavelength than x-rays. Over time, retrieving this knowledge will become more automatic and the acrostic may cease to be needed.

Another example that you may recognise: perhaps as a child you learnt the order of the planets using an acrostic phrase. And now, can you perhaps remember key facts about this sequence without referring to the acrostic? For example, could you quickly say which planet is in-between Mars and Saturn, or which is closest to the sun? If so, this illustrates that such phrases gradually cease to be needed.

Keyword acrostics work in a very similar way to acrostic phrases, but rather than an entire phrase, a single word is used. Each letter of the word is the first letter of a piece of terminology, or some other target item.

An example of a keyword acrostic is the use of the word 'face' to spell out the four musical notes associated with treble clef spaces (F-A-C-E).

## SCENARIO 7.1

Dr A teaches research skills to a group of social science students. He isn't aware of a suitable mnemonic for different research methods, so he has a go at making up his own. He makes up the following keyword acrostic to help students remember the characteristics of case study research: Qualitative, Unusual/unique cases, Interviews/In-depth, Longitudinal, Tests

(spells out 'quilt').

Dr A then tells his students that if they can recall this one keyword, it can be used in their exam to prompt several essential terms. Then, each term can be the basis of a paragraph about case study research.

Many acrostic phrases and keywords are shared on the internet and in textbooks, but if there isn't an obvious one for your course, you can make one up, as the example of Dr A in Scenario 7.1 shows. The example that he came up with shows how a single keyword acrostic can be used to cue an entire essay. These can be very helpful to students in exams.

Another advantage of a single word over a phrase is that there is less chance that students will mix up the order of the items or miss something out (as doing so would involve misspelling the word). However, sometimes it might not be possible to capture the key letters in a single word, in which case, a phrase will be the best option.

## ACTIVITY

Have a think about a set of terms or the steps of a process relevant to your curriculum area. It should be something that students find challenging to remember. You can think of more than one example if you like. Next, highlight or underline the first letter of each one.

Now have a try at writing an acrostic phrase or a keyword acrostic based on the initial letters. It's your choice which one to try – you might want to play around with a few ideas until you find one that fits. Bear in mind that this needs to be both memorable and reasonably simple! You can get some feedback from students, too.

## NARRATIVE TECHNIQUE

A mnemonic approach that many students find intuitive, the narrative technique involves making up a story to include certain key items or learning points. The things that are to be remembered (the apparatus needed for an experiment, for example) function as elements in the story, and the rest of the story is constructed to link these together.

The narrative technique is effective for various reasons. For one, it provides a rich and meaningful context for the items in question, and is often quite visual. In addition, people tend to remember stories and narratives better than they remember facts alone (see Chapter 5). A story also has a specific sequence, making the technique useful for lists where a specific order is important.

However, it's worth bearing in mind that sometimes students may misremember items from the narrative, perhaps retaining the gist of the story but not the details, or substituting semantically similar items when trying to recall it (e.g., remembering 'beaker' instead of 'cylinder' when remembering apparatus for a chemistry practical).

It may also be hard to weave some very technical terms into a meaningful narrative. For example, how do you make 'diffraction' or 'photosynthesis' key points in a story? In such cases, it might be useful for students to substitute a similar-sounding word that would better fit the story. For example, they could replace diffraction with 'defrauding' and photosynthesis with 'photography', perhaps weaving these into a spy story. Even though the words are not the same, they are close enough that they can act as cues to the target term, helping to prompt retrieval from long-term memory.

## ACTIVITY

Write down a set of around five to ten key terms or items relevant to one of your courses. Then, try out the narrative technique using these items as a focus. Or use the set below, each of which are relevant to a physics practical for measuring force and acceleration (a student may need to describe such a practical under exam conditions):

- metre stick (metre-long ruler)
- a toy car
- a pencil
- a pulley and string
- weights
- a stopwatch
- Blu tac.

## THE JOURNEY METHOD

A powerful idea used in a similar way to the narrative technique, the journey method uses the structure of a well-known journey that the student already has in their long-term memory. This acts as a framework for the target items. For example, you could ask students to think about their route from home to school. They have done this so many times, and so actively, that it will be very well stored in long-term memory and easy to retrieve.

Using this journey as a basis, the student then must visually link each item from a list to a step or location along the way to help the item stick in memory. For example, using the apparatus listed in the task above, they could mentally picture a metre stick that has been glued across their front door, a toy car running up/down their front path, a pencil lying on the street outside, a pulley and string hanging from the nearby bus stop, etc. In a history lesson, students might picture key historical characters or artefacts in their mind, linking these to a journey to school or another familiar route in their mind.

Obviously, the specifics will be unique to each student, as they will depend on the kind of home where they live (house, flat, etc.) and what their journey to school is like. As they have created this journey themselves, they are more likely to remember it. The same effect would not work as well if the teacher tried to create the same journey for the whole class using the school corridors.

With this technique (and others – see 'Elaboration', below), the more vividly, actively and unusually the items are linked to the journey, the better. This is known as *elaborative encoding*. For example, it's better to picture a metre stick glued across your door (and then perhaps picture yourself having to limbo dance under it) than just having it sitting propped up against the door. The latter is less vivid and unusual, and more easily forgotten.

When done well, the journey method is a very strong mnemonic. However, there are diminishing returns – most students only have a few journeys that they know really well, so teachers should use it judiciously.

## THE METHOD OF LOCI

The method of loci involves memorising specific items in places within a location. It is a technique with a grand and ancient history; it has been referred to in ancient Greek stories. In more contemporary times, it is a key technique used by 'memory champions' – people who enter competitions and engage in feats of memory such as memorising the order of a deck of cards in a short period of time, and much more. One such individual used the method to accurately remember π to over 60,000 decimal places (Raz et al., 2009).

In a similar way to the journey method (and sometimes the term is used to include both techniques), the method of loci involves the person picturing a set of items in a specific location. Most commonly, a single room is used – perhaps it could be the student's bedroom, a classroom, or the assembly hall at school.

Again, it's best if items are encoded in more elaborated ways, and hard-to-remember terms can be replaced with more everyday equivalents. If a student was trying to remember types of food preservation, for example (chilling, drying, canning, freezing, fermentation, salt, pickling, alcohol, etc.), they could imagine representative items located around their bedroom. Drying could be represented by a hairdryer, pickling by a gherkin, and so on.

# MEMORY PALACE

Rather than memorising items in just one room/location, why not have many rooms where you do the same thing? Creating a memory palace is based around visualising items in real physical spaces, just like the method of loci and journey method. The difference is that it often involves dozens or even hundreds of rooms, with different sets of information connected to each one.

Locations could include every room in a student's house, their school, the homes of their friends, places they go for leisure, and more. As they construct a memory palace, the method of loci can be combined with the journey method, so that each step in a journey is used to link to several different items.

Memory champions who do this competitively will take time getting to know locations and journeys well for this specific purpose, thus preparing for later memorisation. As a teacher, you could do the same. Why not double up an episode of outdoor learning or a school trip into an opportunity to prepare a journey or location for a later mnemonic?

# VISUAL CUES

The examples so far have demonstrated that humans have a very powerful memory for images, something that has been demonstrated in experiments, too. Standing (1973) found that memory for images was very rapid and almost limitless in its capacity.

Images can be used to make a set of study notes more distinctive, helping theories or other ideas to stand out in learners' memory. Consider guiding a class to add eye-catching diagrams or cartoons, especially if these are meaningfully connected to the key learning point, such as an image of suffragettes chained to the railings outside parliament in a citizenship or politics lesson.

The use of visual images in combination with notes is called *dual coding*; there is evidence that this leads to better recall (Clark & Paivio, 1991; see also Chapter 3). At the same time, many learners probably don't do this effectively. They may need to be shown how to use this technique properly, so that images are meaningfully connected to the text and interact with it, rather than just being illustrations.

# MIND MAPS

Mind maps and spider diagrams are commonly used study techniques, but the unfortunate reality is that these are *not* especially effective ways of making notes stick in a learner's mind.

A useful study by O'Day and Karpicke (2021) asked students to study using concept maps, retrieval practice, or both. A concept map is basically like a mind map, but less decorative; it shows related concepts linked together with lines. This study found that while concept mapping can give a short-term boost to performance, this advantage completely disappeared on a test one week later, by which time the concept mappers did *worse* than the retrieval practice group.

Concept mapping also took longer, and even doing both of the techniques had no advantage over retrieval practice alone. This applied to later tests of both facts and meaningful understanding.

Mind maps and concept maps may have their place in education. The initial boost suggests that they might play a role in developing understanding in the classroom. However, they don't appear to be a good bet as a consolidation technique. Instead, the extra time taken to create mind maps and concept maps suggest that they amount to low impact 'busy work', taking up class time in return for little impact.

## RHYMES

How well do you remember the lyrics of your favourite song? Probably quite well! Rhymes aid memory due to the repetitive rhythm, line length and the rhyming pattern of the terminal word of each line. As such, they have been used for centuries. Storytellers in ancient times remembered poems and folk tales without being able to read and write.

There are some famous examples of rhymes used by students, too. You may have heard of the following:

- I before E, except after C, or when sounding like A, like in neighbour and weigh;
- In fourteen hundred and ninety-two, Columbus sailed the ocean blue;
- '59 was the date, when Alaska and Hawaii became new states.

Having said this, coming up with a good rhyme is difficult. Even the famous examples above have elements that could lead to confusion or misremembering. The second one ceases to rhyme if you forget to say that the ocean is 'blue', while pretty much any year (42? 36?) could work in the third example and it would still rhyme.

Overall, students may gain some benefit of using tried and tested rhymes, and they are free to make up their own (the process of inventing them might also help – see 'Generation', below), but it's not a mnemonic that educators should rely too heavily upon.

# POWERING UP YOUR MNEMONICS

It's easy to look at mnemonics and see them as cases of memory doing something unusual. And, of course, mnemonics are designed to stick better in memory than the target items to which they connect. That is their entire purpose.

However, we would rather view these as building on and further illuminating the basic principles of memory described earlier in this book. Why is it that a funny rhyme or story that we make up ourselves is easier to remember than a paragraph from a textbook? There are various reasons, and each principle that mnemonics draw upon can help to deepen your professional understanding of how memory works. We discuss these principles next.

## CUES

Many mnemonics act as cues, helping us recall items via linked information. That is, they provide hints or reminders.

Psychologists have known for a long time that retrieving information from the memory can be hard. There is a lot of information in there; having retained something (so it is stored) does not mean that it will be easy to retrieve (Bjork & Bjork, 2011). We can have the sense of searching around fruitlessly inside our mind, thinking 'I should know this', for example, at a game or pub quiz.

Cues make retrieval easier by providing one key piece of information, such as the first letter. It's a bit like having some of the letters in a crossword clue. Everything can click into place much more easily.

The cue greatly reduces the number of options that the learner has to consider, and therefore makes the search process quicker and easier. We previously discussed how the use of a cue could be helpful when managing the difficulty of a quiz or other retrieval-based task (see Chapter 6).

## LINKING ITEMS

Memory is not just a set of facts but is instead based on sets of interlinked networks called schemas (see Chapter 1). This means that one memory can trigger another. Mnemonics make use of this by focusing on easier-to-remember items to help retrieve more complex ones.

For example, many of the techniques discussed take a complex technical term – the name of a chemical, historical figure, piece of apparatus, etc. – and replace it with something simpler. This simpler item is the focus of the mnemonic. For example:

- in a keyword or phrase acrostic, the item is represented by a cue in the form of a single letter;
- in the journey method, items can be replaced by more everyday objects;
- in some visual techniques, the item is illustrated by or represented by a related image.

This is because memory struggles with complex terminology, and especially with arbitrary information. How are we to remember that Robert Walpole was the first UK prime minister? The name is arbitrary. He could have been called anything! A mnemonic (such as picturing a *pole* jammed into a *wall* in your house) helps to make this easier to retrieve.

## AUTOMATION

Connected with the above idea, and with the point we have made that mnemonics are largely useful as scaffolds, using what you know becomes more automatic over time (see Chapter 2). The more we retrieve it (especially if we do so under spaced and varied circumstances), the easier it becomes to retrieve.

Therefore, over time, it is no longer hard to remember that Robert Walpole was the first prime minister of the UK, or that hydrogen is the first element of the periodic table, or that Edinburgh is the capital of Scotland. These things are (relatively) arbitrary and hard to retrieve at first but become more automatic with time.

In a similar way, number bonds, spelling and other things that learners try to master will become automatic. This is a good thing – it frees up working memory to focus on other things. Achieving that automaticity depends on retrieving the information multiple times over a sustained period of time and in varied contexts.

## ELABORATION

As briefly mentioned above (see 'The journey method'), making a mnemonic more elaborate can help it to stick. Researchers Craik and Watkins (1973) found that examples which made information more elaborate led to better recall, and that this was more effective than just repeating the information. This idea links to the principle that LTM is based on meaning. More elaborate schemas help us to remember more easily because there are more links between the target information and what is already understood.

Elaboration is important when learners re-read their notes. As we have explained in this book, re-reading is a rather ineffective learning strategy. However, it can be made more active and more effective by prompting learners to engage in self-questioning or explanation of key points – in other words, transforming the information they have read in a richly meaningful way.

To make the most of elaboration in their everyday study, learners should attempt to make their examples and mnemonics as vivid as possible. They should think creatively about how ideas could be used, ask themselves questions about the content and engage in discussions.

Elaboration also helps learners to practise the skill of applying the information that they are studying to real-world contexts. Often, this is an important outcome of courses and something that they may have to do in exam situations.

## PERSONALISATION

We remember information better if it is personal to us in some way. This is known as the self-reference effect, and has been widely demonstrated in laboratory experiments. For example, asking participants in a study to answer a question such as 'do you like this thing?' or 'does the word describe you?' appears to lead to better recall than asking other questions about the target items, even questions that promote meaningful processing (Symons & Johnson, 1997).

Some mnemonics are personal because each individual can adapt them to their own interests and knowledge. We can create or choose acrostic phrases, tell stories that fit our interests using the narrative technique, and picture our own homes or journeys when using visual methods.

Personalisation makes sense as a factor in memory because everyone has very good, detailed knowledge about their own lives. The power of basing mnemonics on our knowledge of ourselves illustrates the value of linking new information to well-developed existing schemas.

## EMOTION

Emotional impact also makes mnemonics more effective. You have probably noticed how students in your class will tend remember exciting events or funny things that happen, perhaps retaining these better over the longer term than curriculum content. And who doesn't remember certain key exciting moments in their lives, or when they heard about major news stories for the first time?

Emotion can be a tricky concept to apply in education, as the nature of classroom learning is often fairly routine. It's challenging to guarantee comedy or excitement in class, and attempts to do so can lead to students retaining the wrong message. For example, if students are being taught about Henry VIII and their teacher dresses up to evoke humour and curiosity, students may remember the outfit and not the historical facts!

However, emotion applies well to mnemonics because they can be tailored to the individual. Students can link the method of loci to a place where they have an especially significant memory, or make acrostic phrases that connect to their own individual passions.

The role of emotion in mnemonics is another example of how these techniques are making use of something that is true more widely. Emotions lead to improved attention, and emotional events are retained better in long-term memory (e.g., Conway, 2013), though the reasons for this remain a matter of scientific debate.

## REFLECTION POINT

Think back to your own earliest memories. Can you easily bring to mind childhood events that were especially exciting or unusual? If so, this helps to show the role of emotion in memory.

## SPATIAL LOCATION

Many mnemonics depend to some extent on physical position or location. This helps to illustrate an important feature of LTM, but one that is often overlooked in education – location makes a difference to memory. Doing everything in the same place is not optimal!

In a classic experiment, Smith et al. (1978) set two groups a study task. One completed it in a single room and the other in two different rooms. The group that had studied in two different places later recalled the material better. This clearly contradicts the popular advice to students that they would be best to find one comfortable place and do all their revision there. The opposite is true, at least from a memory perspective: the more learners vary the location, the more effective their study will be.

In school, it may not be possible for teachers to change their teaching location often, but the use of other spaces (e.g., canteen area, outdoors, sports hall, auditoriums, school library) can be built into the curriculum plan, and learners can be encouraged to do the same when studying independently.

Why does this help? New learning is linked to its context. If you study in two different contexts, you are making a broader, richer set of links. These links can then provide cues to recall (rather like how dual coding provides two sets of links, visual and verbal, to help with later recall).

There is an important caveat. If there is something about learning in other locations that impedes study – for example, if the learner feels very stressed and anxious outside their home – then studying in one familiar place may be the lesser of two evils.

However, often, learners will be better served by doing at least some of their study in other places – a friend's home, the school library or on public transport. This is, in effect, a desirable difficulty, making transfer easier at a later date. Despite some of these places not offering perfect peace and quiet, this simply provides another form of variation (another desirable difficulty). After all, the real-life settings where learners may need to later recall and use what they have learnt (the workplace, university or college, the home, etc.) may not always be quiet. Explicitly teaching students about these issues can help them to make better study choices.

## GENERAL MEMORY PRINCIPLES APPLIED TO MNEMONICS

In addition to the specific points made above, there are many broader principles of memory that have been discussed throughout this book, and which – when applied – may make students' use of mnemonics more effective, so that they work even better.
    For example:

- mnemonics depend on active retrieval. Phrases and rhymes won't encode themselves. You need to do something – and it will be more effective to retrieve the mnemonic actively than to (more passively) re-read or highlight it;
- using and encoding mnemonics demands working memory. It therefore takes effort on the part of the learner and the teacher. We can't expect learners to apply the method of loci in the middle of a lesson or activity, for example. They need time to make the most of it along with an understanding of why they are doing it;

- practising mnemonics is going to work better if this practice is spaced out over time, in line with the spacing effect. For example, if learners encounter a new mnemonic for remembering the order of the planets, it would be best to revisit the mnemonic after a delay of a month or two;
- if mnemonics are to support *learning* (rather than performance), we need to give our students opportunities to recall the target information in ways that support real-world recall and use – in varied contexts and applied to new problems. For example, after using a mnemonic to recall the correct order of electromagnetic waves, learners could then tackle some tasks, or engage with a video about ways to measure these waves.

## BROADER USES OF MNEMONIC PRINCIPLES

While we tend to focus on the use of mnemonics for preparing for tests and exams, the same techniques and principles can be applied to many other educational situations. Perhaps you find it hard to remember students' names, or classes tend to miss certain steps when setting up practical work? Any use of mnemonics links to the same essential issue – there is a set of information to be learnt, and the specific wording, detail or order is both important and a struggle to encode.

We will now briefly touch on some of the ways that mnemonic principles can be embedded more widely.

### DURING EVERYDAY TEACHING

We have already seen how memory principles such as retrieval practice and spacing can help to ensure that information is more effectively retained. However, because long-term memory is better with gist than with details, students may remember the broad outline of something (e.g., the idea that cells have various distinct parts) but forget the specifics (e.g., the names and functions of these parts).

Teachers can use their experience and professional judgement to determine which areas of their course content are especially prone to forgetting. It might be helpful to highlight these as a department when planning a unit of work and making newer colleagues aware. Having identified these problem areas, mnemonics present an ideal form of scaffolding for classroom use. Combined with more general strategies to support learning they can be used to break down the target information and make it less daunting to students.

Often, it will be a matter of choosing which mnemonic strategy to use, and this can obviously depend on the nature of the target material. There is certainly no harm in suggesting mnemonic words or phrases (or having learners generate their own), while mnemonic images could be drawn on a whiteboard. Sometimes getting students to generate their own will be effective and memorable. The journey method could be incorporated into outdoor learning or other practical activities.

## TO SUPPORT GOOD NOTE-TAKING

A couple of times in this chapter we have mentioned the quality of students' notes, and the application of mnemonics when they take notes or study from those notes. Of course, note-taking is a key part of independent study and, while good note-taking is not strictly speaking a question of memory, it is worth saying something about how a student's notes can facilitate better memory or undermine it. As teachers we can aim to teach more effective strategies in our lessons. Fortunately, they link to the deeper principles of memory that have been explained throughout this book. There is nothing really new about applying them to effective note-taking; it's just a different context.

First, as noted in Chapter 5, it can be hard for learners to take good notes during certain kinds of tasks, such as practicals, lectures, or videos. This is because working memory capacity is limited and such activities (at least when done with a whole class) often take place at a pace that does not allow them to stop, reflect and take notes of what they have heard or observed as the lesson progresses. For this reason, it is important to build in some time for students to develop good notes later. Also, if learners are to study from the notes, teachers should build in time to check their accuracy.

Note-taking can also facilitate deeper learning and support recall, and this includes the use of diagrams and tables to illuminate and specify important meaningful connections and contrasts. For example, a spider diagram that shows experimental research methods in psychology could help students to see which methods are experimental and which are non-experimental. In a design technology lesson, students might sketch out initial ideas for designing a game or piece of furniture as a table or flow chart.

However, as discussed earlier, the evidence seems to suggest that the benefits of mind mapping or concept mapping are short lived. For longer-term consolidation, notes that promote retrieval would be a better choice. This could include notes taken on index cards, which are ideal for self-testing.

Another option is the Cornell note-taking system. This involves dividing your page into three sections, with a large margin at the side to write the key questions and essential terms, with your more detailed class notes alongside. A section is left blank at the foot of the page to write an overview later and make links to other topics (see image). This very helpfully promotes self-testing, and the summary could be written from memory too.

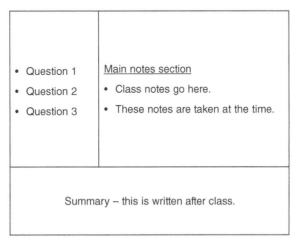

**Figure 7.1**    The structure of a page of Cornell notes

## EVERYDAY MEMORY HACKS

Many of the mnemonic techniques can be used for the more everyday things that we struggle to remember, too. For example, mnemonics could be a very effective way of remembering facts about a hobby or sport. Such tricks are used to good effect by those who play card games to a competitive or semi-competitive level. And as discussed earlier, some of the visual techniques in particular are used by competitive memory experts. It might surprise your students to learn that it is even possible to enter memory competitions! And it might surprise them even more to learn that the people in these competitions aren't born with a 'photographic memory', but that they use the same techniques that you have been working on in class.

Mnemonic techniques are useful for tackling everyday forgetting, too. Many learners forget their jotters, or fail to do their homework, and some may forget other essential duties and items. These situations just show that retrieval from memory is highly fallible. The problem is not getting the information into memory (encoding), but remembering the right thing at the right time (see Chapter 6 for more about 'prospective memory').

Cues are a key strategy for prompting memory and it can be useful for teachers to advise their students that using these is not a sign of having a bad memory, or something to be embarrassed about. There are multiple ways of incorporating them into a daily study or working routine, such as:

- to-do lists to remember and prioritise key tasks;
- diaries and calendars to help with appointments;
- lists and sets of instructions – for example, for safety equipment;
- regular reminders and prompts.

When such things are lacking, learners can (just as with any mnemonics) have a go at creating their own. Using mnemonics fluently and creatively will gradually, over time, become a part of their overall repertoire of study skills.

## A NOTE ON MEMORY TOOLS THAT ARE LESS EFFECTIVE

What about listening to classical music, sniffing essential oils, or using pens of multiple colours? We are sure you have heard these kinds of things suggested as ways to support study habits! Some that we as authors have come across include:

- writing only in purple pen;
- using essential oils to make things better remembered;
- playing the music of Mozart to help you learn better;
- recording your notes and playing them back as you sleep;
- using different stationery for every topic;
- identifying your learning style;
- drinking at least two litres of water per day;
- meditating;
- putting Post-it notes around your home;
- studying only at certain times of day;
- leaving your notes under your pillow.

It would be great if such simple tricks caused things to stick in the memory effectively. However, on the balance of evidence, they are not worth investing time and effort in. Such strategies reflect wishful thinking (or 'magical thinking', as psychologists call it). Even if you can find the occasional supporting study, they can't, on balance, be considered evidence-based study techniques. Rather like superstitions, there is a lack of sound evidence of any cause and effect between these things and better learning.

Unfortunately, students often hear about things that have some tenuous research support, which are then exaggerated or taken out of context. For example, it's true that we can associate smells with memories. However, does that mean that students can associate each piece of content with a different smell, and then somehow sniff these during an exam to help with recall? This has never been demonstrated and would be highly impractical! Sleep has a well-established link to memory, but it is very hard to control; it's therefore hard for students to apply this insight to their study habits.

Overall, students may like to hope that some of the strategies listed above will work, and most won't do any real harm. But it would be far better for them to focus on tried and tested strategies, with effective mnemonics to support the process. As discussed in Chapter 1, a learner may *believe* that something works for them – but they may not be right about this. Part of our job in guiding our students towards more effective learning therefore involves not just telling them that works, but warning against other alternatives that are ineffective and which will therefore distract them and lead to their making poorer use of the time they have to study and revise.

## CONCLUSION

Overall, mnemonics help to artificially boost the retrieval strength of a memory by providing an indirect mental route to that target memory. In the long run, it will be best to use the more direct route and, over time, learners will start to do exactly this because doing so is easier and more efficient. In this sense, a mnemonic is like a crutch or scaffold. It is a temporary support and ceases to be needed over time as knowledge becomes more flexible and automatic.

Mnemonics also illustrate certain features about memory that are often not always obvious. Some of these may only be relevant in some circumstances, but overall, understanding and using these principles can help to make you more effective as an educator. Alongside independent study, such techniques can be applied to classroom learning in order to make tricky bits of content more vivid and memorable, and to learners' note-taking and broader organisational skills, too.

## KEY POINTS

- Mnemonics are techniques used to support memory. They aren't the end goal, but rather act as scaffolding for tricky and detailed sets of information.
- Verbal mnemonics include acrostic phrases, keywords, rhymes and the narrative technique. These can be teacher-provided, but at times it is best if the student generates their own examples.
- Visual mnemonics such as the method of loci and the journey method draw on our very powerful visual long-term memory. Such mnemonics are especially effective if visual images are distinctive and emotive, and it can be worth taking time to 'prepare' a mental space or journey ready for use with a mnemonic.
- Mnemonics can be made more powerful by personalising them – for example, by linking them to a student's own interests, emotions, life experiences and known locations.
- Mnemonics will also benefit from the application of the LTM principles discussed elsewhere in the book, such as actively retrieving them and practising them on a spaced schedule.
- While they are primarily used for exam revision, mnemonics can also be used in the classroom or for everyday reminders.
- Mnemonics and other evidence-informed approaches are much preferable to the 'magical thinking' reflected in some popular approaches to studying.

# 8

# APPLYING MEMORY ACROSS THE CURRICULUM

## INTRODUCTION

This chapter focuses on the differences in how memory principles should be applied across the curriculum. How do key ideas around encoding, consolidation and retrieval apply to maths, English, social subjects, sciences, business studies, languages and so forth? What about PSHE, physical education and creative arts? All of these will be explored, and we will consider the implications of memory for teachers' professional learning too.

Throughout this book so far we have explained the key processes and stores of memory. We have also explored how these apply to classroom tasks, to particular students and to certain types of curriculum content. In fundamental ways, these same stores and processes apply to all aspects of learning, meaning that we can derive from them certain broad educational principles. However, there can be little doubt that different school subjects vary in important ways in terms of how students use their memory. The students in your class will still be using the same memory stores (working memory, LTM, etc.) as in other subjects they study, but the implications will be a little different.

The focus of this chapter is on these differences. Knowledge is structured in different ways across different subject disciplines because they reflect the varied real-world issues studied. The role of automaticity and creativity is different across different disciplines, too (although they do apply to every subject). And it is not always clear that skills operate the same way across disciplines – is the analysis required when studying poetry the same skill as the analysis required when designing a physics experiment, for example? If it is, we should see at least some transfer of the skill from one subject to the other. Practical experience as a teacher suggests that this does not always happen and that students struggle to make links that may seem obvious to the teacher.

In fact, even when commonalities are drawn to learners' attention across the subjects they study, they are often quite bad at applying what they have learnt in new settings. And this is before considering what researchers call *negative transfer* – situations where learning one thing can make you *worse* at another (for example, mistakenly applying the grammar of one language when learning another).

These points suggest that the idea of transferrable skills – often assumed in education and used to justify aspects of the curriculum – should not be taken for granted, and that it would be helpful to think instead about the cognitive principles that will help learners both to retain what is taught and to transfer it more widely, within and beyond the classroom.

You may wish to focus especially on the sections that are most relevant to your own teaching subject(s), but the contrasts with other subjects can be instructive too. And make sure you engage with the section on implications for teacher learning as well!

## HOW WIDELY DO ACADEMIC SUBJECTS VARY?

Before running through the curriculum subject by subject, we should first of all consider where important differences might lie, as well as identifying what we might expect to be the same across all subjects. This will establish the main areas of focus for the chapter, as well as addressing some popular misconceptions about the respective roles of knowledge, understanding and skills.

Although LTM works in rather a similar way for all learners, it does contain different stores, each of which are flexible and can be used for a variety of tasks. In some subjects, building a store of factual information is critical; for others, the ability to make generalisations and use skills creatively may be of greater value.

Exams and assessments, too, vary in their format and this has implications for the kind of preparation that students need, what they will spend time on when studying (e.g., reading vs practice problems) and the mnemonics that will be most helpful.

### ACTIVITY

Briefly take a note of five main ways that students need to use skills and knowledge in *your* subject area. Then read on.

# KNOWLEDGE

It's uncontroversial to suggest that students need to expand their knowledge. This is a key goal of education and, in every subject area or course, learners will come to know things by the end of their course that they did not at the start.

Knowledge about the world is stored in long-term memory in the form of schemas. For example, learners come to know and understand the difference between a solid, liquid and gas in science, to know which authors crafted which novels and poems in English literature and to understand ethical arguments in philosophy or religious studies.

The importance of knowledge is twofold. It is useful for its own sake and it also allows learners to think skilfully and creatively in the subject, to make inferences and argue a point. This is as important in English as it is in science or politics, though the type of information needed may differ.

As discussed in Chapter 7, some information that appears quite arbitrary to learners, such as terminology, can benefit from the use of mnemonics, though examples differ across subjects. Although knowledge in all subjects requires students to form schemas, the precise structure of these schemas differs. For example, in some subjects such as chemistry, the difference between different molecules is generally clear cut and well understood to researchers. In contrast, the difference between international political parties or different styles of novel may have aspects that are ambiguous, or open to debate. In the latter case, the links between concepts within a schema are less clearly organised, and time may be needed to fully explore where the similarities and differences lie.

# SKILLS

Learners don't need to just know the content of their subjects; they also need to *do* things with that new knowledge, such as analyse a poem, solve a calculation, write an essay, or debate a law. Some subjects also require the mastery of specific procedures or sets of steps – for example, the apparatus used in a science lab, gameplans in physical education, or the process of differentiating functions in mathematics. Broadly, we can call these things *skills*.

You have probably come across Bloom's taxonomy of skills at some point in your teaching career (e.g., see Anderson, Krathwohl et al., 2001). This shows skills in a hierarchical diagram, with knowledge and understanding (or 'knowing' and 'understanding') at the bottom, and evaluation and creativity at the top.

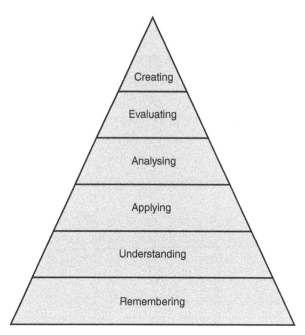

*Source*: Krathwohl et al. (2001).

**Figure 8.1**    Bloom's taxonomy

To some teachers this taxonomy is a key tool, helping them to structure their course and ensure that enough attention is given to skills and their associated command words when planning classes. To others, it is little more than an educational myth, detracting from the importance of factual knowledge. Those who subscribe to the latter view may believe that if we teach factual knowledge, the skills will take care of themselves.

A less controversial concern is that too much of a focus on skills can lead to rather superficial approaches to learning, with a lack of factual knowledge serving nobody. However, too much of a focus on facts can lead to what Perkins and Salomon (1988, p. 22) called 'inert knowledge' – learners know things, but they can't always use their knowledge effectively.

This issue suggests that the division between knowledge and skills is often artificial, and it is unwise to emphasise one excessively at the expense of the other. Knowledge without the ability to use it skilfully and flexibly may be inert. But it's hard to make use of skills without the factual knowledge to back them up. How could you critically analyse a theory if you didn't know the relevant evidence and implications of that theory, for example?

Accordingly, we would suggest placing a focus less on facts and skills and more on *memory and transfer*. This means an emphasis on learners' ability to retain both knowledge and/or skills in memory, tackling forgetting (as discussed earlier, e.g., see Chapters 3–4), and additionally on their ability to later to transfer what they have learnt to new situations. After all, each student needs to have learnt things that last, and they need to be able to use this learning flexibly and in new settings in the future. We would argue that a focus on memory and transfer is more useful than a focus on knowledge and skills (or worse, a focus on just *one* of these two things) because, while essential, neither knowledge or skills are of any use if they are forgotten, or if they cannot be used beyond the classroom.

## AUTOMATICITY

As discussed previously in this book (see Chapter 2, Chapter 7), certain well-learnt information in memory can become almost automatic, thereby reducing the demand on working memory to retrieve or use it. This can occasionally be problematic – for example, when it leads to taking a familiar turning by accident rather than driving the way we intended, or misspellings that became automatic at a young age.

For the most part, though, automaticity is very helpful. Indeed, it is necessary. By reducing the demands on working memory, it frees up a learner's mental capacity to do novel or complex aspects of a task, and considerably speeds up many learning tasks. Again, though, what automaticity might look like can vary across subjects, and the implications of these differences will be considered later in this chapter.

## CREATIVITY

Although it may be considered a skill, creativity deserves some special attention – first, because it is widely considered to be very important – making up the top tier of Bloom's taxonomy, for example, and lauded as a key educational target by major organisations (e.g., WEF, 2016) – but also because it is subject to misconceptions.

One such misconception is that some subjects involve creativity and others do not. This idea has historical origins, Enlightenment scholars rejecting the idea that only God could be creative and recognising art (but only art) as a human creative, pursuit. By the 20th century, psychologists began to recognise that creative thinking works in very similar ways in all subjects, including science and engineering (Sternberg & Kaufman, 2018). Recent research has confirmed that similar basic traits or habits of thought are required for creativity in all areas; these include openness, creative self-efficacy and divergent thinking (van Broekhoven et al., 2020).

However, thinking skilfully and in creative ways also depends on foundational knowledge in the domain (Baer, 2016). As with other skills, it's hard to think creatively if you don't know anything about the issue at hand. It is therefore important that foundational facts and skills are well learnt so that they can be used flexibly and recalled with ease (sometimes automatically), freeing up mental resources to play with ideas and think about the subject matter in new ways.

We will now explore the evidence around how these goals are best achieved across different curricular areas.

## CURRICULUM AREAS AND MEMORY

### ART AND MUSIC

The teaching of art is quite diverse; some elements (e.g., the history of art, analysis of art theory) may have more in common with social subjects (see below). Here, we focus on practical skills and on learning to perceive artwork.

Knowledge and understanding of artistic styles have been quite widely studied. In a classic research study into interleaving, Nate Kornell and Robert Bjork (2008) looked at participants' ability to learn the styles of obscure modern artists. Performance on the task was better when examples were interleaved – such that participants saw several examples from different artists – than when multiple examples by the same artist were shown together.

This research tells us two major things:

1. learning of art styles takes place via induction rather than deduction. We learn by experiencing many examples over a period of time, and gradually develop a mental category for what things belong together;
2. contrast is often more valuable than similarity in this process. That is to say, it's more useful to compare and contrast two dissimilar items than two that belong to the same category. And the more similar the examples are, the more valuable these contrasts are (Carvalho & Goldstone, 2014).

These principles were demonstrated using visual art (specifically, the work of obscure modern painters), but can be applied to other artistic domains such as styles of music or genres of writing. A genre or style is, in effect, a broad category, and within it are multiple sub-categories of specific creators or groups of creators, requiring more specialist knowledge.

What this implies for the classroom is that we should be wary of spending too much class time on a single creator. Merely experiencing a lot of work by one creator is not enough to know everything about them, or to be able to accurately categorise examples in future. Learners also need to know what pieces *don't* belong in this mental category. And that means learning about the broader artistic context.

For example, a session on Spanish 20th-century art would be more valuable to beginner learners than a session just on Juan Miro. Such a session could also broaden their understanding of social influences, history, culture, politics etc., thus elaborating their relevant schemas and making new information less likely to be forgotten.

In music, subtle differences between two pieces or two styles would be more salient if they were played one after the other. This makes the difference much more obvious to the learner, helping them to develop their competence and correctly categorise future examples. However, it's worth noting that what is obvious to one learner might not be obvious to another. Whether differences seem subtle to learners depends on prior learning, and a degree of teacher judgement is required (Firth, 2021).

What about the physical skills involved in art and music? Specific hand movements are retained by procedural memory, a form of long-term memory. You may hear people talk of *muscle memory*, but it is inaccurate to suggest that the memories are retained in the muscles; in fact, they are retained by the brain as schemas (Schmidt & Bjork, 1992).

In addition, musical skills will benefit from many of the desirable difficulties discussed elsewhere in the book. For example:

- variation is more helpful than repetition of the same thing;
- spaced practice works better than overlearning.

An interesting finding from the world of cognitive neuroscience is that procedural memories are better retained after a night's sleep. What's more, memories are more open to 'editing' after sleep, allowing us to refine the skills needed – for example, to improve how well we play a musical piece (Walker et al., 2003).

While art skills such as painting could be compared to things like playing an instrument, it is also a process of composition; in contrast, most musicians are not composing a new piece each time they play. A fuller discussion of creativity is beyond the scope of this book; more on this subject can be read in Smith and Firth (2018), Chapter 4, 'Creativity'. However, overall, the physical skills involved still draw heavily on procedural memory, and benefit from automaticity.

Finally, it is worth mentioning the research into *deliberate practice* carried out by K. Anders Ericsson and colleagues. *Deliberate practice* (henceforth DP) is characterised by being intentional, with focused concentration during the process. It also requires reflection on expert feedback and tends to involve practice which goes beyond the learner's sense of what is comfortable (Ericsson et al., 2007).

The DP framework can help to explain the tendency for learners to plateau. Beyond a certain point, practice alone will cease to result in skills being extended or new skills developed. It is particularly easy to see why this would be the case in the practice of musical skills. Standard repetitive practice leads to automation of flawed habits. DP allows the learner to push themselves and provides focused feedback that can both help to direct further practice and boost their metacognitive awareness of their own limitations.

While DP is only one factor that could affect why one learner is more skilful than another (others could include their starting age, working memory, genetics and personality), it has the benefit of being more easily modified through education.

Overall, DP remains a highly promising approach to improving performance in learning with a strong component of physical skills that can be gradually refined with the aid of feedback, such as artwork and music.

## LITERACY, ENGLISH AND CREATIVE WRITING

Literacy is a major target for educators; learning to read and write is a big topic in itself, more fully covered in other books. However, there is certainly a memory element to the task. Learners have to take in and retain letters, words and other linguistic structures. They must gradually build a vocabulary over time. Coming to use and respond to these is part of what makes us literate, and this process involves increasing automaticity and deepening understanding.

### *Vocabulary*
Learning the meaning of one word is not an 'item' that can be memorised. Rather, for young learners, there will be multiple examples, allowing them to inductively work out when a word can be used and when it cannot. To use language skilfully, we need to know the subtle connotations of a word. While experimental evidence

on this is limited, it seems reasonable to assume that we mainly learn vocabulary through extensive exposure to language in rich, meaningful contexts (Krashen, 2009; Landauer, 2011).

### Spelling

Unlike the meaning and use of a word, spelling can be learnt more directly. There is usually only one correct response. Retrieval practice makes sense here, and is built into popular strategies such as 'look, say, cover, write, check'. However, the spacing effect is probably under-used. If spelling tests and the learning of vocabulary lists are treated as a relatively short-term tasks, the educators will be measuring performance rather than learning.

Creative writing shares many of the same issues discussed under art and, again, we won't venture too far into a discussion of creativity. Suffice to say that creative tasks tend to focus not on single correct solutions but rather a set of possible solutions, some of which will be more successful than others in a given context. The most successful outcome when set the task of writing a short story or poem, for example, depends not just on the author's creativity but also on the expectations of the audience.

It can also be helpful to manage the load on working memory across various writing tasks, not least non-fiction persuasive writing. One way to do so is to pre-teach certain components of the skill and to encourage retrieval of relevant factual knowledge – for example, via a quiz in advance of the creative task.

## PSYCHOLOGY, BUSINESS, PSHE, RELIGIOUS STUDIES AND SOCIAL SCIENCES

In social sciences and related subjects it will be important to have a stock of examples encoded in long-term memory as these will form the basis of essay answers, as well as the learners' ability to think critically and creatively. A key challenge for these subjects, then, will be to develop learners' deep, interconnected knowledge, but also to help them to use it flexibly.

In the case of business studies, for example, factual material to be learnt could include case studies of businesses which have succeeded and failed with their marketing strategies. In psychology, it could include classic research studies which can then be used by learners to support their arguments in an essay. In either case, it is probably relatively easy for learners to develop a basic understanding via a teacher's explanations in class. What is more challenging is to retain details (dates, figures, etc.) in LTM. Doing so can be supported by some of the mnemonics discussed earlier in this book (see Chapter 7).

This group of subjects also places an emphasis on skills such as analysis and evaluation, especially at higher levels of study. In psychology, for example, students won't just need to know *how* an experiment was carried out, but they will also be expected to evaluate that experiment. This challenge can be tackled by scaffolding learners' evaluation skills and using retrieval practice to ensure that fundamental concepts needed to construct this evaluation (e.g., ethical principles in research) are not forgotten. After this, varied examples need to be tackled so that learners begin to use the relevant knowledge with increasing flexibility (so that they can transfer what has been learnt). This should be done over a prolonged period of time, so that we can be confident that students are demonstrating learning rather than performance.

Psychology, business and other social subjects have been widely studied (although for the most part at university rather than school level). Here are some examples of memory-relevant findings from the research.

- A study by Katherine Rawson and colleagues (Rawson et al., 2015) found that interleaved verbal examples in psychology were better remembered than examples that were not interleaved. This demonstrates the value of contrast in the learning process – when developing relevant schemas, learners need to understand not just what a concept is, but also what it is not.
- Zamary and colleagues (2016) found that learners' ability to generate their own examples of concepts was quite poor and that even when given feedback they remained weak. This shows the difficulty of creatively generating material when conceptual knowledge is still being established.
- Rawson and colleagues (2013) used the technique of successive re-learning with a psychology class. This involves combining the spacing effect with retrieval practice. They found that groups who used this scored significantly better on a later multiple-choice test, confirming the relevance of these techniques to this field of study.

Social sciences also challenge their learners to use information in flexible ways. For example, in religious studies, students may need to make critical, reasoned arguments about whether people should access treatments such as blood transfusions which are contrary to their religious beliefs. Critical thinking depends on having a store of knowledge that can be drawn on when thinking (Willingham, 2007).

Similarly, learners need to be able to generalise creatively from prior knowledge and transfer what has been learnt to new and sometimes unfamiliar settings. In a citizenship class, for example, students might be asked to read an article in a newspaper about conflicts around the world and then generate their own opinion on these. They will need to be able to use prior learning flexibly for such a task, suggesting that it should be well learnt via previous tasks which were not only spaced out, but also varied.

Of course, social subjects also overlap to an extent. If students have used source material to back up a point in history, for example, can they then apply the same knowledge and reasoning to a business studies case study? The evidence suggests that such transfer is hard (see Chapter 3), but practice of using their skills in varied ways as well as explicit metacognitive prompts and reminders from the teacher (for example, 'did you look at something like this in history last year?') can help.

## STEM SUBJECTS

Science, technology, engineering and mathematics (STEM) includes some of the most widely researched academic subjects; we therefore have a lot of evidence about them. These areas are often considered especially important by policy-makers and mathematics, in particular, tends to be a mandatory part of the curriculum for a large period of schooling.

Many of the desirable difficulties discussed so far have been tested in a science classroom context. For example:

- interleaved examples were applied to the learning of organic chemistry examples. Eglington and Kang (2017) compared learners' ability to distinguish alcohol molecules from alkyne molecules. When tested after a delay with novel examples, those who had studied interleaved examples performed better;
- misconceptions in science may be reinforced by having them repeatedly retrieved from memory (Stubbs, 2020); teachers should target brief, focused explanations in short bursts to tackle them head on. Providing contrary information is not enough; teachers need to say 'that idea is wrong, and this is why ...' (Will et al., 2019);
- creative thinking plays a vital role in science. The most successful creators – people who come up with new ideas and theories – have excellent domain knowledge (Csikszentmihalyi, 1999).

Science can benefit from fairly clear-cut factual answers and therefore lends itself well to techniques such as quizzing and other forms of retrieval practice. However, it is important to ensure that such information is not separated from its broader context. Instead, learners need to integrate new ideas into their schemas and develop an increasingly interlinked and flexible understanding of the concepts.

Mathematics clearly plays a role across the curriculum, but it also presents some relatively unusual features and challenges. While factual knowledge is important in this subject, it is also highly skills-based and tends to be assessed on the basis of learners' ability to perform tasks and calculations rather than their ability to retain facts. This has implications for how learners should seek to practise.

The importance of skills transferring to other subjects is arguably greater in mathematics because numeracy skills and calculations are fundamental to so many other disciplines, and to everyday life too. For example, learners doing physics might need to calculate the angle of diffraction of light into a prism, drawing not just on their knowledge of the physical properties of light, but also on their ability to apply trigonometry.

Mathematics is therefore a subject where varied practice is critically important. Learners need to retain procedures and use them flexibly. Forms of practice that are too repetitive can be useful for boosting short-term performance but may have less use for boosting long-term learning and transfer.

Some other key findings from research into this domain include:

• interleaving of new statistics concepts can also help learning, having an advantage over blocked learning of such concepts (Sana et al., 2017);
• interleaving is also useful for practice. Rohrer and colleagues (2015) provide evidence that interleaved practice is consistently superior to blocked practice;
• the same idea can be applied to homework; practice assignments can feature some consolidation of newly studied material, as well as some spaced out and interleaved practice of previous types of task.

One way to develop deeper conceptual learning is via tasks that feature *concreteness fading*. This means that the learner begins with concrete examples of maths relationships, perhaps using things like building blocks, quantities of liquid, or tokens. The context is then 'faded out' by moving first to a paper-and-pencil representation, and then to a symbolic representation (Fyfe et al., 2015).

Concreteness fading therefore helps learners to move in steps from the concrete to the abstract. An intermediate level becomes a conceptual bridge, helping them to think their way from specific examples to a more general understanding. This fundamental idea dates back to the work of Bruner (1966), who suggested cycling through three levels of example materials in turn: a concrete 'enactive' form, a pictorial 'iconic' form and a 'symbolic' abstract model or description (see figure below).

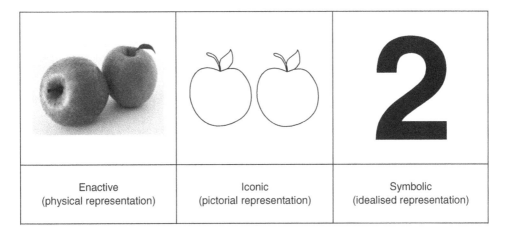

| Enactive (physical representation) | Iconic (pictorial representation) | Symbolic (idealised representation) |

**Figure 8.2**    Ways of representing a concept in more or less concrete forms

*Source*: pxhere.com and publicdomainpictures.net/

**REFLECTION POINT**

Have you tried concreteness fading? Could it work for your own courses and topics? Try brainstorming a few examples of concepts to which it could be applied.

Computing science is part of STEM, but it presents its own unique challenges. As with science, students need factual knowledge that comes easily to mind. But skills such as writing code also have certain elements in common with creative writing and music. Students need to see and understand multiple examples and gain feedback on their own attempts. The process of recognising errors in their own code demands attention, but also draws on a flexible, stored understanding of what commands do that is present in the learner's LTM. Learning to code will benefit from deliberate practice (see Art and music section), while learning concepts such as databases and computer systems depends on an understanding of rules and subtle contrasts that could be developed in the classroom through the use of interleaved examples.

## PHYSICAL EDUCATION

Sports features the learning of procedural memories and, as discussed above (see section 'Art and music'), automation of these skills is an important aspect of learning them. However, in physical education too, learners need to be able to apply skills in flexible new ways. It's not enough, for example, just to be able to shoot a basketball through a hoop, or to be able to roll a kayak. You need to do it at the right moment, and in the context of actual conditions that are a little different every time.

This suggests that learners need to develop memories which are sufficiently flexible and abstract. As with maths learning (see above), they need to be able to analyse a problem and situation, and recognise which skills are relevant. They then need memories of these skills which have not been learnt in a massed fashion in a single context, but through more varied and applied learning.

These points suggest that techniques such as retrieval, spacing, interleaving and variability will again be relevant. A research study by Godden and Baddeley (1975) showed that divers remembered things better in the same context as the items were first learnt. This backs up the idea about studying in varied places (see Chapter 7).

Active learning is also likely to be important; physical education benefits from demonstrations, but it is more valuable to try something out than to have it repeatedly explained or demonstrated to you (Bjork, 1994). However, there is also a 'time for telling', when it comes to issues such as match tactics and strategy. In situations where learners already have a basic understanding, giving information more directly through a briefing is likely to be quicker and more effective than having them develop it inductively (Schwartz & Bransford, 1998).

Some learners may find sports settings to be anxiety provoking, and the sensory input may be overwhelming at times too. Consider, for example, how many classmates might be moving around unpredictably, bouncing balls, and the various sounds of a gym hall. Teachers and instructors could account for this by ensuring that briefings take place in quieter areas and/or by ensuring that learners sit and put down equipment before proceeding with explanations.

## TEACHER PROFESSIONAL LEARNING

Many of the principles discussed so far in this book also apply to teacher professional learning. It may appear that teacher professional learning places the emphasis less on factual knowledge itself, and more on the ability to transfer that knowledge. However, teachers must also retain what they learn – otherwise, what is the point of doing it? (A question that has no doubt crossed many teachers' minds during in-service days!)

However, as with some of the curricular areas discussed earlier (e.g., the generalisation of art styles or concreteness fading in mathematics), the conceptual memory developed should be flexible and relatively abstract. It is of less value to remember specific examples.

Consider, for example, a CPD session where new teachers are shown videos of experienced teachers managing problematic classroom behaviour. The key point would not be that the new teachers remembered the examples that they had seen, but that they retained the broader principles and were able to transfer these principles to their own setting. It may even be misleading to focus too much on a specific case. Novice teachers may fall into this trap, as, in general, novices focus more on the surface features of a problem than on its underlying principles (Hardiman et al., 1989).

This highlights a broader issue: that teacher professional learning, despite often being carried out in highly academic settings, is very practice focused. The specifics of practice are also quite well known in advance. The same doesn't apply to school students, who generally don't know their future career with any certainty. Teachers and teacher educators can predict with a high level of confidence what tasks and skills they will need to engage in, for these are the same workplace tasks and skills that they are already engaging in. They just want to be better at them.

The application of cognitive science to teacher education is less well developed than most of the areas discussed above. However, the points made above emphasise that the main themes of this chapter – memory and transfer – remain relevant. What's more, there is no reason to suppose that desirable difficulties cease to be relevant, or that forgetting ceases to operate. If a teacher is told something at the start of the year, it is highly likely that they will soon forget key details if they don't get a chance to put the idea into practice or do something else to arrest forgetting. Consolidating their learning can make use of strategies such as retrieval practice and the spacing effect.

Halamish (2018) found that both in-service and pre-service teachers failed to predict the benefits of spacing, retrieval practice and interleaving. This suggests that these desirable difficulties are probably being under-used. As with students, teachers may be falling victim to metacognitive illusions, wrongly thinking that easier strategies which lead to faster progress are more effective.

Staff can also attempt to work together as a school to implement memory principles. As highlighted in the EEF (2018) report, it can be helpful if language relating to effective study strategies is used in the classroom. Students benefit from metacognitive talk about memory and learning. If accurate terminology is used throughout the school, it makes it easier for conversations among staff and students to be more precise and productive.

Policies around homework and assessments can also be considered. Scheduling many assessments close together can be problematic, as the pressure on students is very acute. Schools may want to consider when to schedule assessments so that they are not grouped together for all subjects (as this can encourage cramming), and instead find ways to implement regular, low-stakes quizzes and testing.

More broadly, staff may want to ask the question, *'What does (professional practice X) do to improve student learning?'* All too often, the answer is *'Little or nothing'*. Many practices even undermine learning, instead either promoting short-term performance, or wasting staff time for the sake of accountability targets. At the very least, it would behove professionals who purport to care about student attainment to encourage open, professional staff conversations on this issue.

## REFLECTION POINT

This is a good opportunity to reflect back on many of the concepts covered throughout this book. Try to think of ones that could be applied to professional learning in your context, including to your own learning. Perhaps you could flick back through the chapters and begin to make a list.

## CONCLUSION

The basic principles and stores of memory apply across the curriculum. However, there are important nuances, depending on the specifics of the subject and on what kind of tasks learners may need to do in future.

It has been argued in this chapter that an excessive focus on either knowledge or skills can be unhelpful. More importantly, we want to direct educators' attention to thinking about whether what has been studied is likely to be retained in memory, and whether it can transfer to new situations and tasks, including to the workplace.

We have reviewed some of the specific bodies of research most relevant to popular school subjects. Granted, this reflects the research that has been done, and can't reflect other research that could possibly be done in the future. There may be as-yet undiscovered ways to apply the science of memory to curricular subjects. All the same, the advances made by researchers who are interested in these subject areas often represent 'best bets'. This is where the evidence is currently strongest and should be the focus if we wish to remain evidence informed.

Finally, we discussed the application of memory principles to professional learning. What teachers need to learn across their career again has certain key similarities to other areas, but also its own challenges and nuances. Teacher professional learning needs to take account of memory if it is to be effective, and teachers should also consider what they are doing to promote a broader culture of effective practice and effective study skills in their school or college.

## ACTIVITY

Link up with another teacher who teaches a similar area of the curriculum. Where could you pair up to deliver teaching in your own subjects but make specific links across subjects? For example, perhaps a religious studies or citizenship topic about equality could be scheduled for around the time the history department is teaching about votes for women. It will also help if both teachers can highlight the links to their classes, helping students to appreciate areas of overlap on a metacognitive level.

## KEY POINTS

- Knowledge, skills, creativity and transfer are all highly relevant, and teachers should be particularly mindful that what is studied reflects learning rather than performance, and that it transfers to new tasks.
- Arts learning often depends on establishing mental categories through exposure to examples, and interleaved examples appear to be superior here.
- Learning in social sciences depends on deepening knowledge so that learners can construct critical arguments. Techniques for learning concepts via examples can help here.

*(Continued)*

- Language learning depends more on memory than is generally recognised, and strategies for spacing and retrieval practice can be applied to vocabulary. At the same time, language needs to be learnt in context.
- Transfer is especially important in mathematics. Interleaved practice appears to be useful and under-used and, more broadly, maths teaching can benefit from techniques that help students to use skills flexibly in multiple contexts, so that they can better tackle novel tasks.
- Science learning can also benefit from interleaving, as well as retrieval strategies to establish factual knowledge and opportunities for active learning.
- Professional learning by teachers builds on already well-established schemas, but can feature misconceptions. For example, many teachers appear to underestimate the benefits of desirable difficulties.

# REFERENCES

Agarwal, P. K. (2019). Retrieval practice and Bloom's taxonomy: Do students need fact knowledge before higher order learning? *Journal of Educational Psychology*, *111*(2), 189–209.

Agarwal, P. K., & Bain, P. M. (2019). *Powerful teaching: Unleash the science of learning*. John Wiley & Sons.

Agarwal, P. K., D'Antonio, L., Roediger, H. L. III, McDermott, K. B., & McDaniel, M. A. (2014). Classroom-based programs of retrieval practice reduce middle school and high school students' test anxiety. *Journal of Applied Research in Memory and Cognition*, *3*(3), 131–139.

Anderson, L. W. (Ed.), Krathwohl, D. R. (Ed.), Airasian, P. W., Cruikshank, K. A., Mayer, R. E., Pintrich, P. R., Raths, J., & Wittrock, M. C. (2001). *A taxonomy for learning, teaching, and assessing: A revision of Bloom's taxonomy of educational objectives* (Complete edition). Longman.

Arya, D. J., & Maul, A. (2012). The role of the scientific discovery narrative in middle school science education: An experimental study. *Journal of Educational Psychology*, *104*, 1022–1032.

Atkinson, R. C., & Shiffrin, R. M. (1968). Human memory: A proposed system and its control processes. In K. W. Spence & J. T. Spence (Eds.), *The psychology of learning and motivation, Vol. 2* (pp. 89–195). Academic Press.

Baddeley, A. D. (2000). The episodic buffer: A new component of working memory? *Trends in Cognitive Sciences*, *4*(11), 417–423.

Baer, J. (2016). Creativity doesn't develop in a vacuum. *New Directions for Child and Adolescent Development*, *151*(1), 9–20.

Barnett, S. M., & Ceci, S. J. (2002). When and where do we apply what we learn? A taxonomy for far transfer. *Psychological Bulletin*, *128*, 612–637.

Bartlett, F. C. (1932). *Remembering: A study in experimental and social psychology*. Cambridge University Press.

Birnbaum, M. S., Kornell, N., Bjork, E. L., & Bjork, R. A. (2013). Why interleaving enhances inductive learning: The roles of discrimination and retrieval. *Memory and Cognition, 41*(3), 392–402.

Bjork, R. A. (1994). Memory and metamemory considerations in the training of human beings. In J. Metcalfe & A. Shimamura (Eds.), *Metacognition: Knowing about knowing* (pp. 185–205). MIT Press.

Bjork, R. A. (2011). On the symbiosis of remembering, forgetting, and learning. In A. S. Benjamin (Ed.), *Successful remembering and successful forgetting: A festschrift in honor of Robert A. Bjork* (pp. 1–22). Psychology Press.

Bjork, R. A. (2018). Being suspicious of the sense of ease and undeterred by the sense of difficulty: Looking back at Schmidt and Bjork (1992). *Perspectives on Psychological Science, 13*(2), 146–148.

Bjork, E. L., & Bjork, R. A. (2011). Making things hard on yourself, but in a good way: Creating desirable difficulties to enhance learning. In M. A. Gernsbacher, R. W. Pew, L. M. Hough & J. R. Pomeranz (Eds.), *Psychology and the real world: Essays illustrating fundamental contributions to society* (pp. 56–64). Worth.

Bloom, B. S. (Ed.), Engelhart, M. D., Furst, E. J., Hill, W. H., & Krathwohl, D. R. (1956). *Taxonomy of educational objectives: The classification of educational goals. Handbook 1: Cognitive domain.* David McKay.

Bransford, J. D., & Johnson, M. K. (1972). Contextual prerequisites for understanding: Some investigations of comprehension and recall. *Journal of Verbal Learning and Verbal Behavior, 11*(6), 717–726.

Bransford, J. D., & Stein, B. S. (1993). *The ideal problem solver.* Freeman.

Brewer, W. F., & Treyens, J. C. (1981). Role of schemata in memory for places. *Cognitive Psychology, 13*(2), 207–230.

Bruner, J. S. (1966). *Toward a theory of instruction.* Harvard University Press.

Bruner, J. S. (1990). *Acts of meaning.* Harvard University Press.

Burris, C. C, Willey, E., Welner, K., & Murphy, J. (2008). Accountability, rigor, and detracking: Achievement effects of embracing a challenging curriculum as a universal good for all students. *Teachers College Record, 110*(3), 571–607.

Carvalho, P. F., & Goldstone, R. L. (2014). Putting category learning in order: Category structure and temporal arrangement affect the benefit of interleaved over blocked study. *Memory and Cognition, 42*, 481–495.

Clark, J. M., & Paivio, A. (1991). Dual coding theory and education. *Educational Psychology Review, 3*(3), 149–210.

Clinton-Lisell, V. (2019). Reading from paper compared to screens: A systematic review and meta-analysis. *Journal of Research in Reading, 42*(2), 288–325.

Conway, M. (2013). *Flashbulb memories*. Psychology Press.

Craik, F. I., & Watkins, M. J. (1973). The role of rehearsal in short-term memory. *Journal of Verbal Learning and Verbal Behavior, 12*(6), 599–607.

Crehan, L. (2018). *Cleverlands*. Unbound Press.

Csikszentmihalyi, M. (1999). 16 implications of a systems perspective for the study of creativity. In R. J. Sternberg (Ed.), *Handbook of creativity* (p. 313). Cambridge University Press.

Diamond, A. (2013). Executive functions. *Annual Review of Psychology, 64*, 135–168.

Dunlosky, J., Rawson, K. A., Marsh, E. J., Nathan, M. J., & Willingham, D. T. (2013). Improving students' learning with effective learning techniques: Promising directions from cognitive and educational psychology. *Psychological Science in the Public Interest, 14*(1), 4–58.

Dweck, C. S. (2006). *Mindset: How you can fulfil your potential*. Robinson.

Ebbinghaus, H. (1964). *Memory: A contribution to experimental psychology* (H. A. Ruger & C. E. Bussenius, Trans.). Dover. (Original work published 1885).

Education Endowment Foundation (EEF) (2018). *Metacognition and self-regulated learning: Guidance report*. educationendowmentfoundation.org.uk/public/files/Presentations/Publications/Metacognition/EEF_Metacognition_and_self-regulated_learning.pdf

Eglington, L. G., & Kang, S. H. (2017). Interleaved presentation benefits science category learning. *Journal of Applied Research in Memory and Cognition, 6*(4), 475–485.

Ericsson, K. A., & Kintsch, W. (1995). Long-term working memory. *Psychological Review, 102*(2), 211–245.

Ericsson, K. A., Prietula, M. J., & Cokely, E. T. (2007). The making of an expert. *Harvard Business Review, 85*(7/8), 114–121.

Farrell Pagulayan, K., Busch, R. M., Medina, K. L., Bartok, J. A., & Krikorian, R. (2006). Developmental normative data for the Corsi block-tapping task. *Journal of Clinical and Experimental Neuropsychology, 28*(6), 1043–1052.

Firth, J. (2021). Boosting learning by changing the order and timing of classroom tasks: Implications for professional practice. *Journal of Education for Teaching, 47*(1), 32–46.

Francis, B., Taylor, B., Hodgen, J., Tereshchenko, A. & Archer, L. (2018). *Dos and don'ts of attainment grouping*. www.ucl.ac.uk/ioe-groupingstudents

Fyfe, E. R., McNeil, N. M., & Borjas, S. (2015). Benefits of 'concreteness fading' for children's mathematics understanding. *Learning and Instruction, 35*, 104–120.

Gathercole, S. E. (1999). Cognitive approaches to the development of short-term memory. *Trends in Cognitive Sciences, 3*(11), 410–419.

Giebl, S., Mena, S., Storm, B. C., Bjork, E. L., & Bjork, R. A. (2021). Answer first or Google first? Using the internet in ways that enhance, not impair, one's subsequent retention of needed information. *Psychology Learning and Teaching, 20*(1), 58–75.

Godden, D. R., & Baddeley, A. D. (1975). Context-dependent memory in two natural environments: On land and underwater. *British Journal of Psychology, 66*(3), 325–331.

Halamish, V. (2018). Pre-service and in-service teachers' metacognitive knowledge of learning strategies. *Frontiers in Psychology, 9*, 2152.

Hardiman, P. T., Dufresne, R., & Mestre, J. P. (1989). The relation between problem categorization and problem solving among experts and novices. *Memory and Cognition, 17*(5), 627–638.

Hausman, H., & Kornell, N. (2014). Mixing topics while studying does not enhance learning. *Journal of Applied Research in Memory and Cognition, 3*, 153–160.

Howard-Jones, P. A. (2014). Neuroscience and education: Myths and messages. *Nature Reviews Neuroscience, 15*(12), 817–824.

Kornell, N., & Bjork, R. A. (2008). Learning concepts and categories: Is spacing the 'enemy of induction'? *Psychological Science, 19*, 585–592.

Krashen, S. (2009). Does intensive decoding instruction contribute to reading comprehension? *Knowledge Quest, 37*(4), 72–74.

Landauer, T. K. (2011). Distributed learning and the size of memory: A 50-year spacing odyssey. In A. S. Benjamin (Ed.), *Successful remembering and successful forgetting: A festschrift in honor of Robert A. Bjork* (pp. 49–70). Psychology Press.

Loftus, E. F. (1996). *Eyewitness testimony*. Harvard University Press.

Mayer, R. E. (2003). The promise of multimedia learning: Using the same instructional design methods across different media. *Learning and Instruction, 13*(2), 125–139.

Maylor, E. A. (1996). Age-related impairment in an event-based prospective-memory task. *Psychology and Aging, 11*(1), 74–78.

Miller, G. A. (1956). The magical number seven, plus or minus two: Some limits on our capacity for processing information. *Psychological Review, 63*(2), 81–97.

Morehead, K., Rhodes, M. G., & DeLozier, S. (2016). Instructor and student knowledge of study strategies. *Memory, 24*(2), 257–271.

Nairne, J. S., Thompson, S. R., & Pandeirada, J. N. S. (2007). Adaptive memory: Survival processing enhances retention. *Journal of Experimental Psychology: Learning, Memory, and Cognition, 33*(2), 263–273.

Neisser, U. (1967). *Cognitive psychology*. Prentice Hall.

Newton, P. M., & Salvi, A. (2020). How common is belief in the learning styles neuromyth, and does it matter? A pragmatic systematic review. *Frontiers in Education, 5*, 602451.

O'Day, G. M., & Karpicke, J. D. (2021). Comparing and combining retrieval practice and concept mapping. *Journal of Educational Psychology, 113*(5), 986–997.

Perkins, D. N., & Salomon, G. (1992). Transfer of learning. *International Encyclopedia of Education, 2*, 6452–6457.

Piaget, J. (1950). *The psychology of intelligence*. Routledge.

Pintrich, P. (2002). The role of metacognitive knowledge in learning, teaching, and assessing. *Theory into Practice, 41*(4), 219–225.

Rawson, K. A., Dunlosky, J., & Sciartelli, S. M. (2013). The power of successive relearning: Improving performance on course exams and long-term retention. *Educational Psychology Review, 25*(4), 523–548.

Rawson, K. A., Thomas, R. C., & Jacoby, L. L. (2015). The power of examples: Illustrative examples enhance conceptual learning of declarative concepts. *Educational Psychology Review, 27*, 483–504.

Raz, A., Packard, M. G., Alexander, G. M., Buhle, J. T., Zhu, H., Yu, S., & Peterson, B. S. (2009). A slice of π: An exploratory neuroimaging study of digit encoding and retrieval in a superior memorist. *Neurocase, 15*(5), 361–372.

Roediger, H. L., & Karpicke, J. D. (2006). Test-enhanced learning: Taking memory tests improves long-term retention. *Psychological Science, 17*, 249–255. doi.org/10.1111/j.1467-9280.2006.01693.x

Rohrer, D., Dedrick, R. F., & Hartwig, M. K. (2020). The scarcity of interleaved practice in mathematics textbooks. *Educational Psychology Review, 32*(3), 873–883.

Rohrer, D., Dedrick, R. F., & Stershic, S. (2015). Interleaved practice improves mathematics learning. *Journal of Educational Psychology, 107*, 900–908.

Rohrer, D., & Taylor, K. (2006). The effects of overlearning and distributed practise on the retention of mathematics knowledge. *Applied Cognitive Psychology, 20*(9), 1209–1224.

Rosenshine, B. (2012). Principles of instruction: Research-based strategies that all teachers should know. *American Educator, 36*(1), 12–19.

Salomon, G., & Perkins, D. (1988). Teaching for transfer. *Educational Leadership, 46*(1), 22–32.

Sana, F., Yan, V. X., & Kim, J. A. (2017). Study sequence matters for the inductive learning of cognitive concepts. *Journal of Educational Psychology, 109*(1), 84–98.

Sanchez, C. A., & Wiley, J. (2006). An examination of the seductive details effect in terms of working memory capacity. *Memory and Cognition, 34*, 344–355.

Schmidt, R. A., & Bjork, R. A. (1992). New conceptualizations of practice: Common principles in three paradigms suggest new concepts for training. *Psychological Science, 3*, 207–217.

Schuman, H., Walsh, E., Olson, C., & Etheridge, B. (1985). Effort and reward: The assumption that college grades are affected by quantity of study. *Social Forces, 63*(4), 945–966.

Schwartz, D. L., & Bransford, J. D. (1998). A time for telling. *Cognition and Instruction, 16*(4), 475–522.

Shibli, D., & West, R. (2018). Cognitive load theory and its application in the classroom. *Impact: The Journal of the Chartered College of Teaching, 2*.

Simons, D. J., & Chabris, C. F. (2011). What people believe about how memory works: A representative survey of the US population. *PLOS One, 6*(8), e22757.

Simons, D. J., & Chabris, C. F. (2012). Common (mis) beliefs about memory: A replication and comparison of telephone and Mechanical Turk survey methods. *PLOS One, 7*(12), e51876.

Smith, M., & Firth, J. (2018). *Psychology in the classroom: A teacher's guide to what works*. Routledge.

Smith, S. M., Glenberg, A., & Bjork, R. A. (1978). Environmental context and human memory. *Memory and Cognition, 6*(4), 342–353.

Soderstrom, N. C., & Bjork, R. A. (2015). Learning versus performance: An integrative review. *Perspectives on Psychological Science, 10*(2), 176–199.

Standing, L. (1973). Learning 10000 pictures. *Quarterly Journal of Experimental Psychology, 25*(2), 207–222.

Sternberg, R., & Kaufman, J. C. (Eds.) (2018). *The nature of creativity*. Cambridge University Press.

Stubbs, A. (2020). *Minimising misconceptions through the design of explanatory sequences*. my.chartered.college/impact_article/minimising-misconceptions-through-the-design-of-explanatory-sequences/

Swaffer, M. A. (2019). Seductive details in educational materials: Exploring attention distraction using eye tracking. Doctoral dissertation, University of Northern Colorado. UNCO Digital Archive.

Sweller, J. (1990). Cognitive processes and instructional procedures. *Australian Journal of Education, 34*(2), 125–130.

Symons, C. S., & Johnson, B. T. (1997). The self-reference effect in memory: A meta-analysis. *Psychological Bulletin, 121*(3), 371–394.

Tulving, E. (1985). Memory and consciousness. *Canadian Psychology/Psychologie Canadienne, 26*(1), 1–12.

Tversky, A., & Kahneman, D. (1974). Judgment under uncertainty: Heuristics and biases. *Science, 185*(4157), 1124–1131.

van Broekhoven, K., Cropley, D., & Seegers, P. (2020). Differences in creativity across art and STEM students: We are more alike than unalike. *Thinking Skills and Creativity, 38*, 100707.

Walker, M. P., Brakefield, T., Hobson, J. A., & Stickgold, R. (2003). Dissociable stages of human memory consolidation and reconsolidation. *Nature, 425*, 616–620.

Will, K. K., Masad, A., Vlach, H. A., & Kendeou, P. (2019). The effects of refutation texts on generating explanations. *Learning and Individual Differences, 69*, 108–115.

Willingham, D. T. (2007). Critical thinking: Why is it so hard to teach? *American Educator, 31*, 8–19.

Willingham, D. T. (2009). *Why don't students like school?* Jossey-Bass.

Wittrock, M. C. (1974). Learning as a generative process. *Educational Psychologist, 11*(2), 87–95.

World Economic Forum (WEF) (2016). The future of jobs: Employment, skills and workforce strategy for the fourth industrial revolution. *Paper Presented at the Global Challenge Insight Report.* WEF.

Zamary, A., Rawson, K. A., & Dunlosky, J. (2016). How accurately can students evaluate the quality of self-generated examples of declarative concepts? Not well, and feedback does not help. *Learning and Instruction, 46*, 12–20.

# INDEX